THE *Embroidery* HANDBOOK

All the Stitches You Need to Know to Create Gorgeous Designs

Dhara Shah

creator of Chain_Stitch

PAGE STREET
PUBLISHING CO.

PAGE STREET
PUBLISHING CO.

First published in 2021 by
Page Street Publishing Co.
27 Congress Street, Suite 105
Salem, MA 01970
www.pagestreetpublishing.com

Distributed by Macmillan, sales in Canada by The Canadian Manda Group.

25 24 23 22 21   1 2 3 4 5

ISBN-13: 978-1-64567-444-3
ISBN-10: 1-64567-444-4

Library of Congress Control Number: 2021931945

Cover and book design by Molly Kate Young for Page Street Publishing Co.
Photography by Chris and Meghan Thompson; step-by-step photos by Dhara Shah

Printed and bound in the United States of America

THE
Embroidery
HANDBOOK

DEDICATED TO MY BABIES KESHAV AND KABU,
AND MY ROCK, HIMANSHU

TABLE OF CONTENTS

INTRODUCTION

My earliest embroidery memories are from my childhood: seeing the women around me—aunts, neighbors, employees of my parents—spending their evenings together, embroidering in the traditional styles of Gujarat, my native state on the west coast of India. While they were busy gossiping, their fingers would weave magic. Most of their pieces were huge—more than a yard (meter) at least—and would take anywhere from one to six months to complete. Unlike the pace of life outside, time was not of importance here, and what they created would go on to become an heirloom—something that would get passed down to their grandchildren one day. And that for me has always been the essence of embroidery: putting a bit of your soul into creating something that outlasts you.

I have embroidered on and off my entire life, and I love how accessible of a craft it is. The basic supplies needed are widely available, easy to carry and quite cheap. While I traveled from one part of the country to another, either to study or for work, my embroidery supplies came with me, neatly packed in a small bag. It is good to keep creating, even on the go!

In this book, I hope to pass on my love for embroidery, which is interwoven through all the aspects of my life, to you. With this comprehensive guide, you'll learn about sourcing and selecting supplies, as well as basic techniques like transferring patterns. You'll also learn to master fifteen carefully selected essential stitches, which are enough to complete any project of your choice. There are full-color, step-by-step photographic tutorials to help you learn each of these stitches. You'll then be able to put them into practice with the many projects that cover different themes and include detailed instructions and schematics. I've intentionally arranged the stitch tutorials and projects to build on each other, so you can get the hang of the basic embroidery elements before moving on to something slightly more complex. As little cherries on the top, the entire book is peppered with top tips to make your experience of learning embroidery even easier.

The projects are small enough that you will be able to wrap up even the most complex ones in just a couple of weeks. However, I have also included some patterns that can be traced in a tiled and staggered fashion, like the Lotus Outline Pillowcase (page 133) and Autumn Breath Tote Bag (page 125) to create bigger pieces should you wish to experiment! There are also patterns you can use individual elements of separately (Fishy Playdate [page 56], Autumn Breath Tote Bag [page 125] and Springing It Table Runner [page 121]).

Thirty years of my life have been steeped in embroidery, and in the last five years, I have turned this erstwhile hobby into a successful business and gained a lot of support and appreciation from the craft community around the world. I have amassed a large social media following on my Instagram account @chain_stitch where I document my daily embroidery journey. I have published multiple patterns in reputed craft magazines all over the world and collaborated with renowned fellow artists. For me, this book is a way of sharing all that knowledge I have painstakingly accumulated over the years! My dearest wish when you are using this book is for you to find the embroidery process made easier so you can begin to reap the benefits of this wonderful craft without the usual trips and stumbles. I hope you create your own heirlooms that can be cherished by yourself and your loved ones and create wonderful memories with the passage of years.

Sharashah

GETTING STARTED

Any new endeavor is daunting, including a hobby! There are so many choices, one doesn't quite know where to start. So, first up, we will tackle where to source the basic materials to get you started on your embroidery journey and how much to get in the initial run. You will also learn how to secure the fabric to your embroidery hoop, transfer a pattern, separate floss strands without the ever-frustrating tangling, secure your floss ends and finally, how to close your embroidery hoop to get a beautifully finished embroidery piece!

SOURCING THE RIGHT MATERIALS

There is no end to how your supplies can pile up once you are really immersed in a hobby! However, you don't want to invest too much of your hard-earned money buying items that aren't necessary to have at the onset. In this section, I will cover the basic supplies you'll need to get started, as well as some supplies that aren't exactly necessary but will make the embroidery process easier for you in the long run. Fabric, embroidery hoop and floss are the three cornerstones to creating a great embroidery piece, so I've included extra helpful details in these sections for you!

I recommend starting with a pure cotton fabric (or if you want to go a little more exotic, linen) in either solid colors or soft prints. These are the easiest materials to embroider on—they have a tough weave, thickness and zero elasticity. While it is certainly possible to embroider on other fabrics, it's better to gradually scale up to working with these.

When sourcing fabrics to practice your stitches, I recommend rummaging through your own home to find an old plain pillowcase or a tea towel you can practice on. You can also visit a local fabric wholesaler, which usually has offcuts going for less than a dollar. While these are too small for larger sewing projects, they are perfect for beginner embroidery projects. Another good option is your local thrift store—you can usually come across table or bed linens for a steal! Look for fabric that has no elasticity and a strong weave (the horizontal and vertical weave lines should be tightly closed in) and is opaque. Then check the tag to make sure it's 100 percent cotton or linen, and make sure whatever you select is big enough for the project you have in mind. To purchase brand-new fabric, look for reputed brands such as DMC, Anchor and Zweigart.

TIP: Your fabric should measure roughly 2 to 3 inches (5 to 8 cm) larger than your pattern size. So, for a 6-inch (15-cm) project, you want fabric that is a minimum of 8 inches (20 cm).

Different varieties of hoops

EMBROIDERY HOOPS

Embroidery hoops come in a variety of sizes, shapes and materials, but they all hold the fabric in the same way—sandwiched between an inner ring and outer ring. What differs is how the fabric tension is created. The most common hoop is one with screw tension, where a screw on the outer hoop lets you adjust the tension on the hoop. Both DMC and Elbeese wooden hoops are excellent quality. Another popular option is the flexi hoop, which is made of vinyl that fits tightly over a plastic inner hoop. I prefer to use these to frame a finished project rather than embroider with them, as they don't give the flexibility of adjusting the hoop's tension. Good-quality plastic hoops also give you very good tension while being available in a variety of bright colors.

Regardless of the hoop you choose, it needs to hold the fabric taut and give good tension. Otherwise, your embroidery will not sit well on the fabric and might pucker it, distorting the design. Make sure there is no gap between the inner and outer hoop, which will affect the tension. Also check the frames for internal cracks.

Embroidery hoops are available in craft stores and through online vendors like Etsy and Amazon. When you are still new to the craft, I recommend buying them in person so you can check the quality. Once you know a brand or a shop that works well for you, it is fine to buy them online. I recommend getting two or three hoops in different materials to get a feel for what you're most comfortable working with. The size will be determined by your project.

TIP: Get an embroidery hoop that is about 1 inch (2.5 cm) bigger than your project size and another that is exactly your project size—the larger hoop will help you embroider the edges of your project easily and then transferring your project to the right size hoop will make it sit pretty!

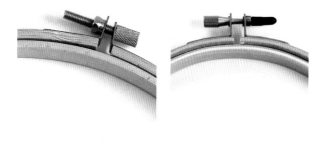

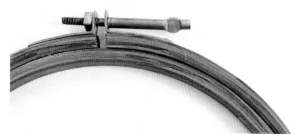

Top left: Inner and outer rings with gap.
Top right: No gap between rings.
Bottom: Ring with cracks.

For me, floss is where you let your imagination run wild! I prefer name-brand flosses to their cheaper counterparts because they fray less, and when used on apparel or homeware, the colors are fast and the floss holds up to repeated washing. My favorite brands are DMC (they have an amazing range of about 500 colors, textures and shade palettes to choose from) and Anchor.

Floss comes in a variety of types: cotton stranded, Pearl Cotton, tapestry wool, linen and so on. All give different results based on their weave, but cotton six-stranded "skeins" and Pearl Cotton are the most common kind used by crafters the world over. The six-stranded floss can be divided into smaller groups of strands or used as is for a chunkier feel. For the sake of consistency, I have made all the projects in this book with DMC six-stranded floss. You can also use Pearl Cotton floss, which is not divisible but comes single-stranded in several thicknesses distinguished by numbers (3, 5, 8 and 12). I normally substitute two strands of stranded floss for one strand of Pearl Cotton No. 8 floss.

All the floss from standard companies have a unique identifier number—this allows you to correctly reorder a floss you have run out of! You can get floss from your local craft store or online, though I also love sourcing it from small local businesses. If you're a beginner, I recommend getting a good variety of single-color skeins. Over a period of time, you will develop a color palette that speaks to you and that you will tend to navigate toward.

Different varieties of floss

Unique identifier numbers in branded floss

Different types and sizes of needles

NEEDLES

Embroidery needles—sometimes called crewel needles—are widely available and generally have larger eyes than sewing needles, which make it easier to thread the floss. A needle with a big enough "eye" that is sharp enough to pierce your fabric without puckering is perfect! Needles vary by size, which is indicated by their number; the larger the needle number, the smaller the needle. So, if you are using multiple strands of floss or Pearl Cotton floss for your embroidery, you want to use a lower-numbered needle, for example a size 3, and to embroider with only two or three strands of stranded floss, a size 5 needle is sufficient. While these are the two needle sizes we'll use in this book, I recommend buying a pack of needles with roughly ten different sizes so you can then decide which size works best for you. Most craft stores will stock these at quite a reasonable price.

TIP: If you end up working on multiple projects at some stage, avoid at all costs leaving the needle in the fabric. High humidity and the inherent quality of the needle can end up leaving permanent rust marks on the fabric. Always store your needles in a pin cushion or a needle box after using them.

SCISSORS

Any sharp pair of scissors, roughly 3 to 4 inches (8 to 10 cm) long, will do the job, including the standard pair of snips you get at your local superstore. There are embroidery aficionados (like me!) who have a collection of beautiful embroidery scissors in different colors and designs, though, so by all means, get a pretty pair if you like.

TIP: Get a pair of scissors with a sharp end (a lot of craft scissors have rounded edges) in case you need to pull out the stitches; this feature will help you do it more neatly.

Different types and sizes of scissors

TRANSFER PEN

Transfer pens are used to trace the embroidery pattern onto your fabric, and unlike with regular pens, you can easily erase the pen marks after the embroidery is made. You'll want to get two pens: one for light-colored fabrics and one for dark-colored fabrics.

For light-colored fabrics, a simple pencil can be used in a pinch, but I prefer a more specialized transfer pen like the heat-erasable Frixion pen. Like its name suggests, you can remove the pen marks using a hair dryer or an iron, though it sometimes leaves white residue marks on certain fabrics. So try it on a small corner of your fabric first. Another popular transfer pen is the water-erasable pen in blue or black, but I don't use it a lot because it requires your entire embroidery to be washed, dried and then recentered on your hoop. If your embroidery is very detailed, this can cause puckering.

To transfer on dark-colored fabric, a simple white-colored pencil can be used, though they aren't the easiest to use on fabrics. Another option is a white water-soluble pen, though my favorite so far is the Bohin Extra Fine Chalk Mechanical Pencil.

TRANSFER PAPER

Sometimes, you can't trace your pattern directly on the fabric for various reasons—the fabric texture is too chunky or uneven or the fabric is really thick and opaque (denim, for instance). Transfer papers to the rescue! There are a variety of transfer papers, including water-soluble stabilizers. You can trace the pattern on these stabilizers, fix them on your fabric and once your embroidery is done, you wash off the stabilizer with warm water. There's also standard dressmakers' carbon paper, which you can use to transfer patterns on difficult fabrics like denims. They are coated on one side with a powdery, colored ink that will wash out of the finished piece. You can get them in both dark and light colors. Rather than stocking up on transfer papers when you're first starting off with embroidery, I recommend beginning with fabrics that are easy to transfer on using a transfer pen. Once you graduate to experimenting with your embroidery, invest in a transfer paper that is suitable for your current project.

Iron-On Transfer Pen

White Water-Erasable Pen

Bohin White Chalk Mechanical Pencil

Water-Erasable Pen

Heat-Erasable Pen

Self-Erasing Pen

Different kinds of transfer pens

Carbon paper and water-soluble stabilizer

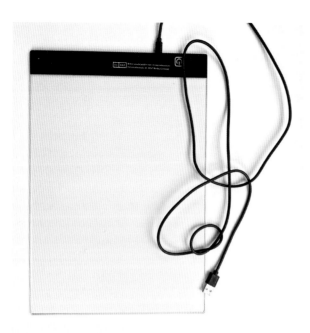

Lightboard

Top: Fabric fixed too loosely in the hoop.
Bottom: Fabric fixed taut in the hoop.

LIGHTBOARD

A lightboard is an extremely useful gadget that makes pattern tracing easier, especially when the fabric is dark or opaque and the pattern is intricate! See "Transferring the Pattern" (page 19) for more information. You can purchase reasonably priced lightboards in local craft stores or on Amazon for as low as $15.

TIP: If you are using a particularly thick and/or dark fabric, try tracing using a lightboard at night, with the rest of the lights off.

BASIC TECHNIQUES

This section covers the steps you need to complete before starting your actual embroidery. You will learn how to correctly fix the fabric on your hoop, separate floss strands, thread your needle, transfer the pattern and close your hoop securely.

FIXING THE FABRIC ON THE HOOP

When getting ready to fix the fabric in the hoop, do not unscrew the screw on the outer hoop completely. Keep it so that the outer hoop is snug enough to hold the inner hoop in place but loose enough that it can slip in and out.

Place the inner hoop on a flat surface. If you plan to trace the pattern on the fabric, place the fabric wrong side up. Don't worry if the fabric sags into the center. Place the outer hoop over the fabric, centering the hoop carefully. Gently press the outer hoop down over the inner hoop, and gradually tighten the screws until taut. You can always adjust the tension at a later stage.

Once you have traced the pattern (see "Transferring the Pattern," page 19), unscrew the screws, remove the fabric from the hoop and put it back right side up and centered. You can use the circular hoop marks on the fabric to help you put it correctly on the right side. Make sure it's snug enough to avoid puckering.

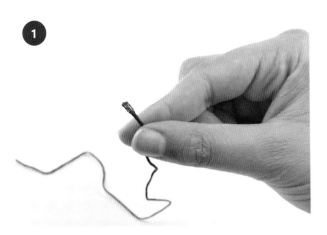

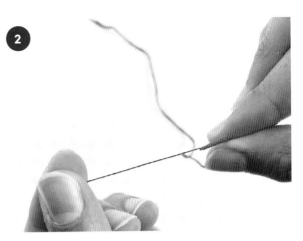

TIP: Gently tap your knuckles on the stretched fabric; you should hear a low drum-like sound. That is your cue that the fabric is stretched well on the hoop.

SEPARATING THE FLOSS STRANDS

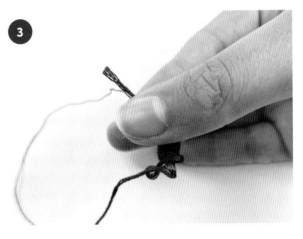

Using divisible floss lets you change the texture of your embroidery by increasing or decreasing the number of strands of floss. However, separating floss can become a headache if you don't do it the correct way. The regular DMC/Anchor floss has six strands in one bunch. You can remove the number of strands you want to stitch with one at a time and then put them back together using these steps:

1. Cut the length of thread you want to use. Grip the thread between your first finger and thumb and gently tap on the protruding edge of the thread. That will separate the strands in your fingers.

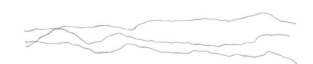

2. Grab one strand from the bunch while holding the rest between your fingers firmly enough that they don't fall and gently enough to pull the single strand through. *Don't* try to pull more than one strand at a time or you will tangle the entire bunch. Without letting go of the bunch, pull out the one strand.

3. As you pull, you'll notice the rest of the threads bunching under your fingers, but don't let it alarm you. As soon as you have a strand loose, the rest of the bunch will fall into place!

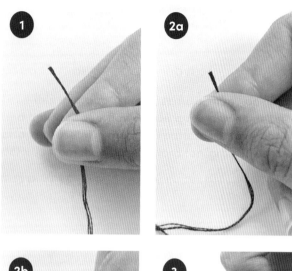

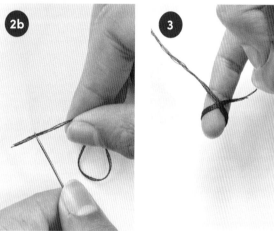

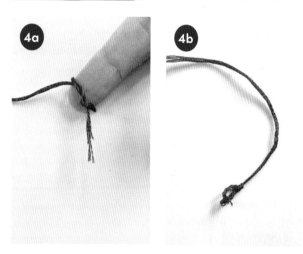

4. Repeat the process and keep the separated strands aside; once you have the required number of strands, align them and thread them into the needle together.

THREADING THE NEEDLE AND SECURING THE FLOSS

Many stitchers find it challenging to thread the needle, and people use multiple techniques to succeed. Here's my preferred method:

1. Snip off the scraggly ends of the floss and lick them. This will stiffen your thread.

2. Hold the thread between your thumb and forefinger, and pull it back until only a little end is visible. Place the needle on top of your thread and slide the needle through.

3. Next, you need to knot one end of the floss so it will not pull through the fabric while stitching. Wrap the thread around your index finger, making an X as shown, leaving around ½ inch (1.3 cm) of floss end.

4. Using your thumb, "roll" your floss end over the other diagonal of the X and gently pull it off your fingers to form a knot. Cut off any extra floss beyond the knot.

You can also use a needle threader if you prefer.

Using a needle threader.

TRANSFERRING THE PATTERN

There are several methods for transferring patterns, and every artist has their favorite. For tricky fabrics, I prefer using a stabilizer; otherwise, I use a lightboard.

Method 1: Trace directly onto the fabric with or without a hoop in place.

This is the simplest and easiest method, though you'll need to be able to see the pattern clearly through your fabric's opacity. Do it in a well-lighted room, sitting down, with a chair and table. Center and fix the fabric right side down on your hoop. Turn the hoop upside down, place it on your pattern, aligning the edges, and slowly trace the pattern, moving the hoop around along with the pattern if required. Unscrew the hoop, remove the fabric and place it right side up. You can also trace your pattern without a hoop, with the fabric facing right side up. Do this when your pattern is too big to fit within your hoop.

Method 2: Trace against a window.

If your fabric is opaque or dark colored and you are unable to see the pattern through it, an easy way to trace is by keeping it against a bright window during the daytime. As in Method 1, center and fix the fabric right side down on your hoop. Turn the hoop upside down, place it on your pattern and put the whole contraption against a clean window and trace. To keep your pattern in place, you can stick your hoop to the pattern using paper tape. Unscrew the hoop, remove the fabric and place it right side up (as in Method 1), making sure to center it carefully. Now you're ready to go!

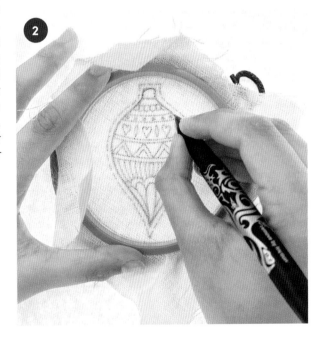

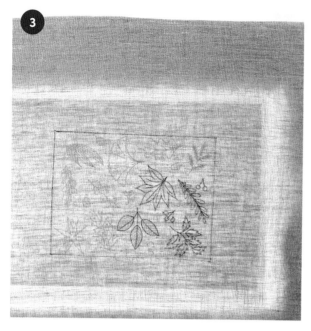

Method 3: Trace using a lightboard with or without a hoop in place.

I recommend investing in a basic lightboard to make your pattern visible against a dark or opaque fabric (see "Sourcing the Right Materials," page 11). The process for tracing is the same as Method 1, with the only difference being that you place the lightboard at the bottom, followed by the pattern in the middle and the upside down hoop right on top.

The lightboard is very useful when you are transferring a pattern onto already-stitched items like cushions or bags, since these have two stitched layers you need to navigate. To transfer a pattern without a hoop (say, onto a cushion or a bag), simply insert the lightboard inside your bag or cushion, with the pattern in between and the fabric side you want to trace on top.

Method 4: Transfer using carbon/tracing paper.

If you want to transfer your pattern onto a stitched homeware item that is very thick and dark (for example, denim) where even a lightboard won't be effective, another alternative is carbon paper (see "Sourcing the Right Materials," page 11). Carbon paper is best for patterns where you plan to fill up the entire design with embroidery (instead of just outlining the design), as it doesn't erase easily without a thorough washing. Do a transfer and wash on a sample fabric before using it on your good fabric.

Put the fabric right side up on a solid surface, with the carbon paper in the middle and the pattern printout on top. Trace the pattern using a pencil.

Method 5: Using an iron-on pen transfer method.

This is very similar to the carbon paper method, except instead of tracing your pattern on carbon paper, you use an iron-on pen to transfer your design onto the fabric. This method works best for symmetrical designs, where the front and the back of the design look the same. Trace the pattern onto a light piece of regular or tracing paper using the iron-on transfer pen. Turn the design upside down, facing the fabric, and center it where you want it to transfer onto the fabric. Put your iron off the steam setting and on medium heat, then gently run it over the pattern (or as per the instructions on your transfer pen)—it will take 45 to 60 seconds for the pattern to transfer fully. Note that the transferred pattern will be lighter than with other methods.

Method 6: Transfer using a wash-away stabilizer.

If your standard transfer methods aren't working, your saviors are stabilizers! Cut the stabilizer paper in the shape of (but a little bigger than) your pattern, transfer the pattern using a regular pen and then fix it on the fabric. Some stabilizers are adhesive and can be stuck on fabric, some can be fixed using an iron, and for those that have neither of these options, simply fix them in place using a running stitch on the edges. All the stabilizers come with detailed manufacturer instructions on how to make the transfer. Once you have stitched your pattern, simply wash it off with warm water and let your fabric air dry.

SCHEMATICS

Schematics are the blueprints that help you translate a pattern into a perfect embroidery design. They can be represented with either a black-and-white or colored sketch. Most schematics give you information about the floss numbers you need to use, the stitches and the number of strands for each element that you need to embroider. Follow the schematic alongside the instructions methodically and your embroidery will come to life in front of you!

CLOSING AND BACKING THE HOOP

Closing the hoop is the process of trimming and tucking away the excess fabric once you are done with the embroidery, giving it a beautiful finished look. If your embroidery needs to be washed before this final stage, remove it from the hoop, wash it and hang it to air dry without wringing it. Once it is fully dry, iron on the back side to remove the creases. Then carefully center and fix the embroidery on the hoop, making sure it is taut. Although there are many ways to back a hoop, here are two methods that I usually use:

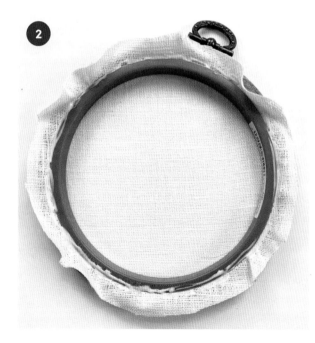

GLUING YOUR EMBROIDERY FABRIC TO THE HOOP

1. Turn your hoop backward as shown in the photo. Trim around the excess fabric, leaving just ½ to 1 inch (1.3 to 2.5 cm) of fabric.

2. Using fabric glue or any glue safe for fabric, apply it evenly to about ¾ inch (2 cm) of the fabric length and stick it to the hoop. A lot of artists use hot glue. Move on to the next ¾ inch (2 cm), and so on, thereby completing the whole hoop. As shown in the photo, apply the glue on the outer edge of the ring, so any excess does not spill onto your embroidery area.

OPTIONAL: Once the glue has set, you can cut a circular piece of felt the size of the inner hoop and stick it on top of this if you want your hoop back to be hidden.

SEWING THE HOOP BACK

1. Trim the excess fabric around the hoop, leaving around 1 inch (2.5 cm). Thread a needle with enough thread to go all the way around the circle. Tie a large knot at the end. You can choose a thread the same color as the fabric. For the illustrations, I have chosen a contrast thread so it shows clearly.

2. Sew around the edge of the excess fabric with large running stitches (see page 26 for a running stitch tutorial). The stitches should be about ½ inch (1.3 cm) from the fabric edge.

3. When you reach the beginning of the stitches, pull the thread to gather the edges in toward the center. Take a back stitch or two (see page 27 for a back stitch tutorial) to secure the gathering, and then tie a large knot close to the fabric.

OPTIONAL: You can cut a circular piece of felt the size of the inner hoop and glue it on top of this if you want your hoop back to be hidden. Alternatively, you can sew the felt piece with a blanket stitch (page 44).

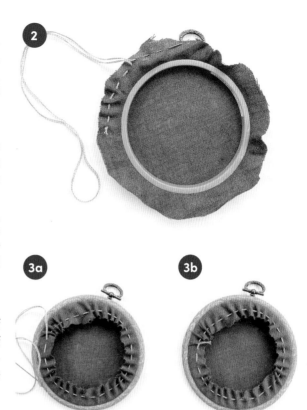

LEARNING THE STITCHES

Now that you're all sorted with your fun embroidery supplies, are you ready to dive into the magical, calming world of embroidery stitches?

There are hundreds of stitches to learn from around the world, some of which are so simple you will wonder how you did not already know them and some that will take you a few days to master. That process itself can get daunting and leave you bewildered. Which stitches should you learn first? Which stitches can be substituted for others? What are the best stitches for embroidering borders? How do I make texturally rich embroidery? With so many questions, it's easy to get lost and give up. Believe it or not, though, you don't need to master hundreds of stitches to make beautiful patterns. In this section, I cover fifteen basic stitches you can use to make just about any element in any project that strikes your fancy. They can be used for a variety of functions, like borders or outlines, to fill up empty spaces around the design and to fill inside an embroidery space. I have included easy-to-learn but versatile stitches like chain stitch and back stitch. There are texturally rich stitches like bullion knots and woven wheel rose. The stitches become easier the more you practice them, and the projects in the book are meant to give you exactly the practice you need to master these stitches. I recommend practicing all the stitches except French knots and woven wheel rose with three strands of floss. French knots and woven wheel rose give the best results with six strands.

I recommend you try out at least one project featuring each of the stitches. With time, you will, like all crafters, end up with your stock of favorite stitches that you are most comfortable embroidering (mine is chain stitch, little surprise!). But it's good to start off trying to learn and practice as many as possible. So let's get stitching! I am so excited, and I hope you are, too!

RUNNING STITCH

Difficulty Level: Easy

Used For: Outline, filling

One of the quickest and easiest stitches to work with, running stitch is the ideal stitch to start learning embroidery. This versatile stitch can be used to fill up different elements or simply for making outlines.

TOP TIP: Make the stitch on the right side of the fabric slightly longer than the stitch on the wrong side to create a filled-in effect.

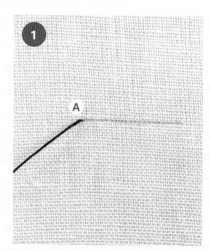

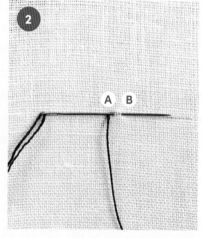

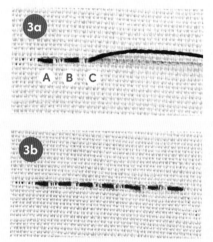

1. Bring the thread to the front of the fabric at A. (If you are stitching as an embellishment outside the boundary of a stitched design, then bring the thread parallel to the edge of the pattern. We will do this for Snowy Christmas Trees, page 102.)

2. Make a small stitch from A to B, approximately 1/16 inch (2 mm), taking the needle beneath the fabric along the line.

3. Pull the thread through the fabric at C. Make another small stitch as before, making sure the stitch is the same length as the previous stitch. (If you are stitching outside the boundary of a stitched design, keep the stitches parallel to the lines of the design.) Continue in the same manner until you reach the end of the line.

BACK STITCH

Difficulty Level: Easy

Used For: Outline, filling, stems, accents (leaves and flowers)

Along with chain stitch, I consider the back stitch to be the backbone of hand embroidery because it lends itself to so many uses: as an outline for borders and stems and for filling in! It is very easy to master this stitch, and we will use it in a single stitch pattern (Fishy Playdate, page 56) as well as in more complex patterns. I loved the effect of using back stitch in filling up leaves in the Autumn Breath Tote Bag project (page 125) as well as an outline stitch in the adorable Fishy Playdate pattern (page 149).

TOP TIP: To make the perfect back stitch, *always* take the needle back through the same hole that the previous stitch emerged from. This will get easier with practice.

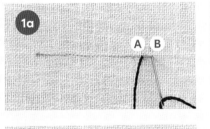
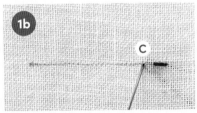

1. Bring the thread to the front of the fabric at A, a short distance inside the edge of the pattern line. Make a small stitch, taking the needle down through the fabric at B, at the beginning of the pattern. Re-emerge at C and pull the thread through the fabric. The distance from A to C should be the same as the distance from A to B.

2. Take the needle back down at A, making sure it's through the same hole in the fabric. Re-emerge at D, keeping the distance the same. Pull the thread through the fabric.

3. Keep stitching following steps 1 and 2.

STEM STITCH

Difficulty Level: Easy

Used For: Stems, outlines

The texture of stem stitch makes it quintessential for stitching—guess what?—stems! Try embroidering lines of stem stitches adjacent to each other to get a corded effect. Although I rarely embroider entire projects with just stem stitch, I have to admit I loved using just the stem stitch to embroider The Chakra Chronicles (page 61) and the Lotus Outline Pillowcase (page 133); stem stitch is so regal, it makes every project you use it in shine.

TOP TIP: A fun thing to try is to combine two different gradients of the same color floss (two strands each) and try making stem stitches with this mix to see the lovely shading effect you get without using variegated floss! (Variegated floss is shaded floss—the shading can be across different colors or as different gradients within a single color. We will be using variegated floss in multiple projects in the book.)

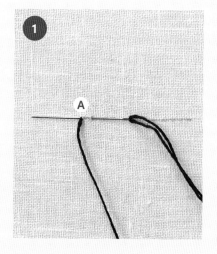
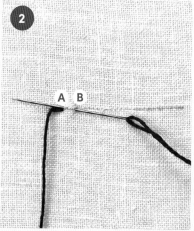
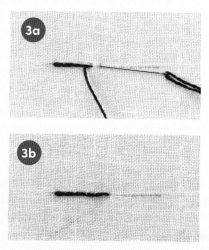

1. Take the needle to the front of the fabric at the edge where you want to begin the embroidery. With the thread sitting below the needle, make a back stitch to the front of the edge from A. Pull the thread through the fabric.

2. Again with the thread below the needle (this should always be the case with stem stitch), take the needle from B to A and pull the thread through the fabric using the same hole that A created.

3. Keep making stitches in this manner. To end the stitch, take the needle to the back of the fabric at the last stitch but do not re-emerge. Secure the thread with a little knot at the back.

SATIN STITCH

Difficulty Level: Easy

Used For: Filling

Satin stitch is easy to understand, yet so many people find it daunting. This is because they're not flattening the floss as they make the stitches or they're starting at the wrong point in the pattern, which makes the stitch direction go wrong. To help you avoid this, I've included a couple of tips here, as well as in the Falling for Feathers pattern on page 69. Adjusting the number of floss strands you use will change the texture of this stitch considerably, so play around and see the textures of your elements evolve!

TOP TIPS: When you make a stitch using multiple strands, make sure the strands sit evenly (and not intertwined) on the fabric—this will give the true "satin" feel. You may need to smooth it out with your fingers after every few stitches. If you are embroidering a particularly large area using satin stitch, you might struggle to keep your stitches parallel—I highly recommend drawing parallel reference lines on your fabric with a pencil to guide you while you make your stitches. The reference lines will hide under the stitches so you don't need to worry about removing them. (I have done this in multiple projects in this book, including Kitty on My Books [page 82] and The Blue Door of My Dreams [page 87].)

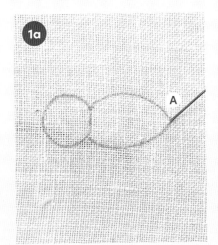

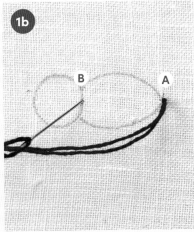

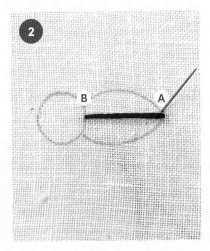

1. When embroidering a curved or a complex shape using satin stitch, begin near the center and bring the thread to the front of the fabric at A. Take the needle to the back of the fabric at B, directly along the line of A and along the shape. Pull the needle through.

2. Re-emerge close to A and take the needle back through the fabric near B, parallel to the earlier stitch and leaving a narrower space between the stitches.

(continued)

SATIN STITCH (CONTINUED)

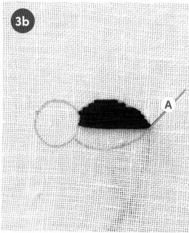

3. Pull the thread through the fabric to complete the second stitch. Continue working the stitches in the same manner. When one half is filled up, take the thread to the back of the fabric and embroider the second half, bringing the needle out at the other side of A.

4. When working satin stitch for a straight shape (like a square or rectangle), follow the same steps as above, except begin at one edge of the shape and end at the other in one go.

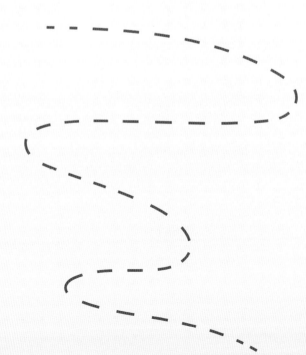

CHAIN STITCH

Difficulty Level: Easy

Used For: Outlines, filling; use detached chain stitch (single chain stitch) for leaves and daisies

Chain stitch is one of the most versatile stitches—it is great to fill up leaves and petals and works equally well for outlines! This is my personal favorite stitch (hence the name of my Etsy shop CHAINSTITCHSTORE and Instagram handle @chain_stitch!) because, when done well, very few stitches look as finished as chain stitch does. And it can give shape to so many patterns such as wheat sheafs, sunflowers and daisies, just to mention a few.

TOP TIP: Although I love small, neat chain stitches, a whole school of people go for longer stitches. And they look great as well—just keep your floss a little thicker than usual and you'll be able to carry off longer chain stitches, too.

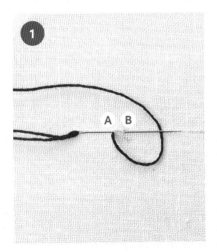

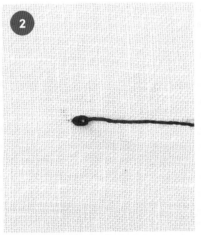

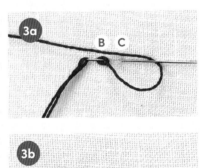

1. Bring the thread to the front of the fabric at A and pull the thread through. Take the needle from A to B using the same hole in the fabric at A. Loop the thread under the tip of the needle at B.

2. Pull the thread through until the loop lies snug around the emerging thread like a single link in a chain (hence the name chain stitch!). Take care not to pull the thread too tight to avoid snagging the entire stitch.

3. Make another stitch, taking the needle through the same hole in the fabric at B and re-emerging at C. Ensure the thread is under the tip of the needle. Pull the thread through as pictured and continue working the stitches.

4. To finish, make the last stitch and take the needle to the back of the fabric. Tie a knot at the back of the fabric.

FRENCH KNOTS

Difficulty Level: Intermediate

Used For: Flower centers, filler elements, filling spaces

All the knot stitches have a bad reputation for being very difficult to execute, but once you get the technique clear in your head, you will be surprised by how easy these stitches are to master! And they are a must-have in your arsenal because they are instrumental in adding that much-needed texture to your project. I have used French knots plentifully across different projects in the book, notably the Welcoming Spring Flower Bouquet (page 97), Snowy Christmas Trees (page 102) and Sprinkles on my Donut (page 72) to name a few. They add that little bit of sophistication in my projects.

TOP TIP: Use French knots scattered in your designs to act as space "fillers" in your florals, much like you would use baby's breath in your floral arrangements!

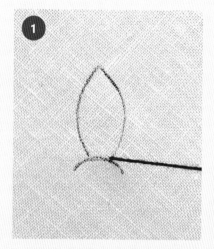
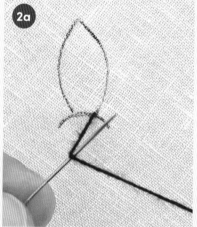

1. Bring the thread to the front of the fabric. Hold the thread firmly with your thumb and index finger on your nondominant hand about ¾ inch (2 cm) away from the fabric.

2. With your dominant hand, bring the thread over the needle. Make sure the needle points away from the fabric. Wrap the thread around the needle once. Keeping the thread taut, begin to turn the point of the needle toward the fabric.

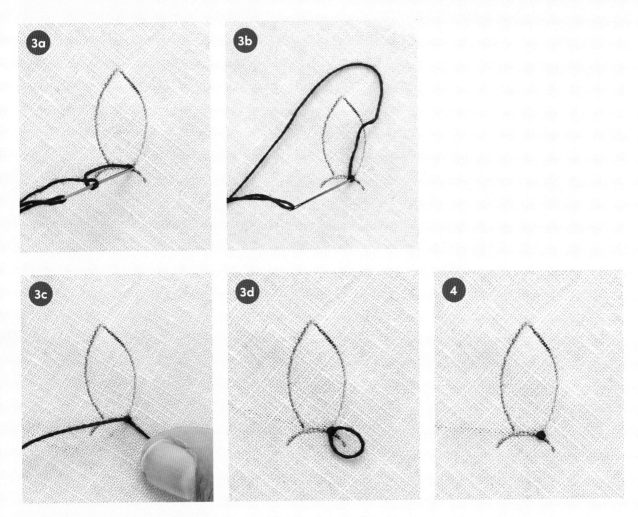

3. Pierce the needle into the fabric 1 to 2 fabric threads away from the emerging thread and gently slide the knot down the needle into the fabric in a continuous motion. Pull the thread until the knot is firmly around the needle. Slowly push the needle to the back of the fabric while holding the knot in place under your thumb. Begin to pull the thread through the fabric.

4. Continue to pull until the thread disappears under your thumb and is completely pulled through. You have completed your French knot.

SPLIT STITCH

Difficulty Level: Easy

Used For: Outline, filling, adding raised textures for satin stitch

Part of the stem stitch family, split stitch is a very old stitch dating back to English medieval times, when it was popular as a filling stitch. Nowadays it is used for both outline and filling in patterns, and visually it looks quite similar to chain stitch. As a filling stitch, it tends to be quite time consuming; however, the final result looks very delicate and refined!

TOP TIPS: In my opinion, the split stitch works the best using a single divisible floss, like Pearl Cotton or woolen yarn, because it is easier to pierce just that one single floss instead of multiple stranded ones.

Make a border using split stitch before making your satin stitch to get a chunkier satin stitch texture.

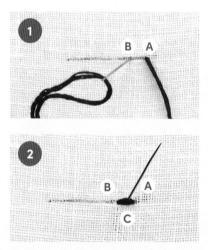

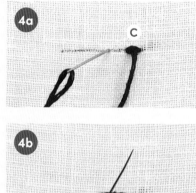

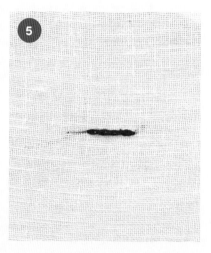

1. Bring the needle out of the fabric at A at the beginning of the pattern and make a small stitch, taking the needle back through the fabric at B. Pull the thread through.

2. Bring the needle out of the fabric at C, piercing the thread of the previous stitch, roughly halfway between A and B.

3. Pull the thread through the fabric to complete the first stitch.

4. Take the needle to the back along the stitch line, approximately 3 millimeters from C. Pull the thread through the fabric and re-emerge through the center of the second stitch.

5. Continue working stitches in the same manner.

BULLION KNOTS

Difficulty Level: Intermediate

Used For: Roses, textural elements, floral centers

Bullion knots used to be my Everest! I could never get it right—until I realized that I was doing the technique all wrong! This is another stitch that gives a 3D aspect to your embroidery while being quite sturdy at the same time (unlike, say, the woven wheel rose). This makes it a perfect raised stitch to use for functional items such as clothing.

TOP TIP: I strongly recommend using a milliner's needle for this stitch. A milliner's needle has the same thickness across its length, which makes it easier to pass the wound-up thread through the needle.

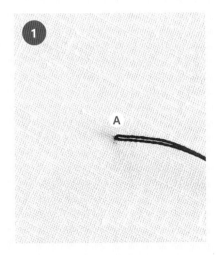

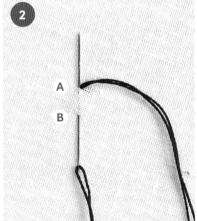

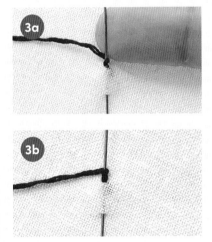

1. Bring the needle out through A and pull the thread through the fabric.

2. Take the needle to the back of the fabric at B and re-emerge at A. Take care not to split the thread. The entire thread should sit either on the left of the needle or on the right.

3. Raising the needle a little bit, start wrapping the thread clockwise (if it was sitting on the right of the needle) or counter-clockwise (if it was sitting on the left). Keeping the point of the needle raised, pull the initial couple of wraps firmly down onto the fabric. Work the required number of wraps, making sure that you pack them in evenly and tightly.

(continued)

BULLION KNOTS (CONTINUED)

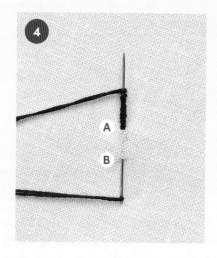

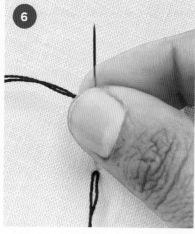

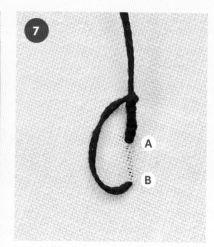

4. For a straight bullion knot, keep the distance of the wrap the same as the distance from A to B.

5. For a curved bullion knot, such as for a rose petal, keep the distance of the wrap a little longer than the distance from A to B.

6. Then, holding the wrapped thread with your thumb, ease the needle through the fabric and the wraps gently.

7. Keep pulling the needle until the wraps lay completely against the fabric, on the side of A.

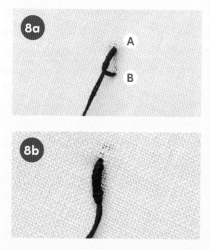

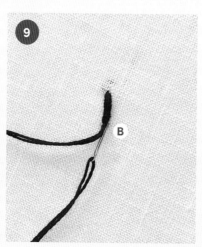

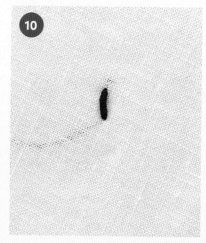

8. Slowly turn the needle and the looped floss toward B while gently laying the loop flat against the fabric. The extra floss will get pulled through.

9. Adjust and straighten the wraps with the back of your needle if required and put the needle back through the fabric at B to finish your knot.

10. Finished bullion knot (straight).

HERRINGBONE STITCH

Difficulty Level: Easy

Used For: Filling leaves and petals, borders

Herringbone stitch has been used in folk embroidery arts for many generations and gives any pattern an unbeatable folksy vibe! It's also one of the few filling stitches that can double as a cool, thick border stitch. You can make the herringbone really closed in (as in this tutorial) or space out the stitches (making sure to always keep the distance even) for a more latticed look. I find the herringbone stitch to be an excellent replacement for satin stitch when you want to embroider items of functional use; unlike satin stitch, it doesn't snag quite so easily and has a longer shelf life!

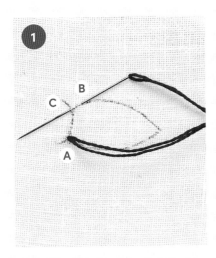

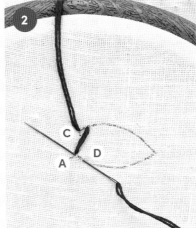

1. Bring the needle out of the fabric through the first stitch line at A. Now, take the needle in through B, which lies diagonally across A on the second stitch line. Then take the needle *backward* out of the fabric through C, lying on the same stitch line as B but parallel to A. Pull the thread through the fabric.

2. Repeat step 1 except now on the first stitch line. Take the floss from C diagonally across the fabric to D on the first stitch line and bring the needle backward toward A. The distance from where you bring the needle out near A should be very small and uniform for a lovely herringbone pattern.

3. Continue to make such crosses on both stitch lines alternately. Make sure the diagonal stitches are parallel to each other and the adjacent stitches are even to bring out the best look.

4. When working an asymmetrical curved shape, always start at the broad end and head toward the tapered end of the pattern.

WOVEN WHEEL ROSE

Difficulty Level: Easy

Used For: Flowers, textural elements

This stitch produces a magical effect with a big WOW factor. And yet, it is one of the easiest stitches to execute! If you want to give a 3D feel to your embroidery project, woven wheel rose is the way to go. I have made this stitch the hero in my wreath pattern "Life Is Beautiful" (page 92)–check it out to see how the woven wheel roses pop out of the frame!

TOP TIP: Use two or even three different shades of the same color to give the stitch an ombre effect. Use two completely contrasting colors to give a pop.

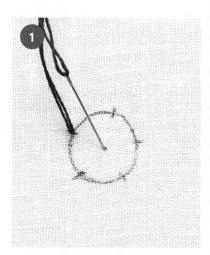
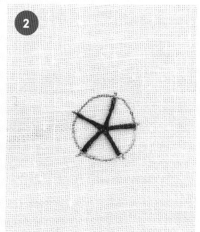

1. In your template's circular shape, mark the center with a dot. Mark five dots along the circumference, imagining the circle as a pentagon. Next, using thread, bring the needle to the front of the fabric at one of the outer edge marks. Take it to the back at the center of the circle.

2. Pull the thread through the fabric, then continue to work straight stitches from all the remaining outer edge marks to the center of the circle in the same manner to make "spokes." Secure the thread at the back of the fabric and cut it if you want your petals to be a different color. If you are making the petals using the same floss, do not cut the thread after securing the back.

3. To make the petals, bring the floss to the front of the fabric between two spokes as close as possible to the center. Working in a counterclockwise direction, weave the floss over and under alternate spokes of the framework until one round is complete. We won't be piercing the fabric at all until we are ending the stitch.

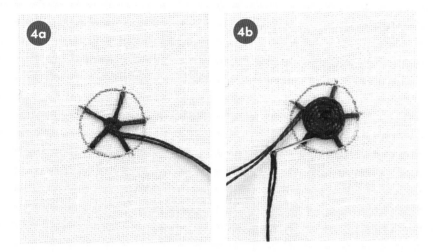

4. Pull the needle firmly (but not too tightly) so the framework does not show at the center. If you are making this flower with a single floss color, keep working rounds in the same manner, using looser tension than before, maintaining the over-and-under sequence until the entire framework is completely hidden. If not, take two or three more rounds and take the needle to the back of the fabric and secure it.

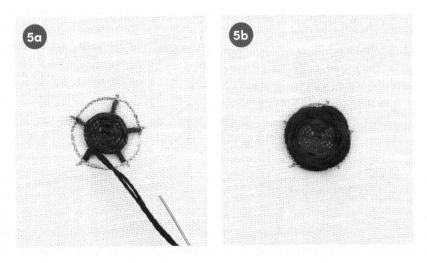

5. Take another floss color and emerge next to where the previous thread went to the back of the fabric. Using looser tension, continue weaving until the entire framework is completed. Take the needle under a spoke to the back and secure the floss at the back of the fabric.

OPTIONAL: You can embroider some French knots in a contrast color with six strands of floss at the center if you want to add another dimensional element to this flower.

STEM STITCH ROSE

Difficulty Level: Intermediate

Used For: Roses, textural elements

This stitched floral motif gives a beautiful texture associated with the stem stitch, but in the form of a rosette! It is perfect to use when you want to make a lot of small roses (see The Blue Door of My Dreams [page 87]) but don't want to spend the effort required in making tiny satin stitches or bullion knots, the stitches normally used to embroider roses. Just as I prefer using the herringbone stitch over the satin stitch when embroidering functional use items like cushions, I also prefer using the stem stitch rose instead of the woven wheel rose for these items.

TOP TIP: Use two or more colors to embroider this rose—it creates an ombre effect with aplomb!

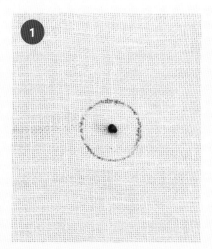

1. To make the center of your rose, take your preferred (either darkest or lightest) shade of floss and make a French knot.

2. To make the inner petals, bring the needle to the front of the fabric at A near the French knot and pull the thread through.

3. Take the needle to the back of the fabric at B and re-emerge at C (very close to A), keeping the thread below the tip of the needle, just like you would for a stem stitch. Pull the thread through to complete the first stem stitch.

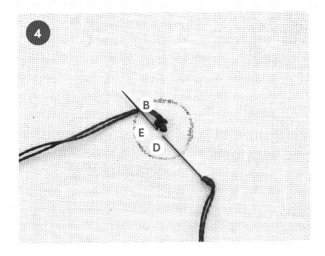

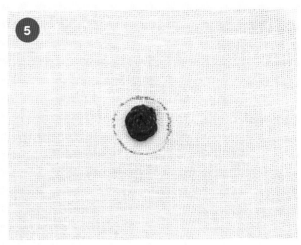

4. Take the needle to the back of the fabric at D and re-emerge at E, close to B, and pull through the fabric.

5. Keep working stem stitches in this manner, completing four or five rounds of stem stitches.

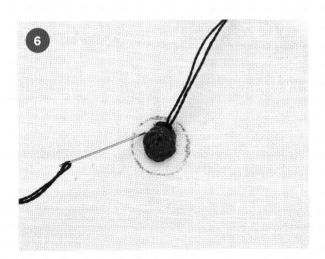

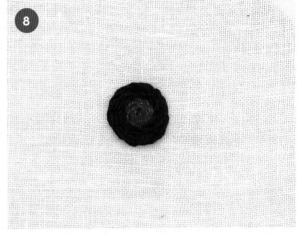

6. To make the outer petals: Change your floss to the next darker/lighter shade if you're using different colors. Bring the needle to the front of the fabric, halfway along and on the outside of the last stitch you ended, so as to make a stem stitch.

7. Work three or four more rounds using stem stitches as shown in steps 1 through 5.

8. Pull the floss through the fabric and end the stitch at the back of the fabric. Take the darkest/lightest shade (if you're using more than two shades) and complete another three or four rounds (until the entire framework is covered) to complete the stem stitch ribbon rose.

GRANITOS STITCH

Difficulty Level: Easy

Used For: Buds, cactus leaves

I call this the "bud" stitch because, in my opinion, no other stitch captures the textures and delicacy of a flower bud quite as well as the granitos stitch. However, this stitch is also very useful in mandala patterns or for embroidering plump cacti leaves. Granitos is derived from the Spanish word for "grains," as this stitch resembles plump grains.

TOP TIP: Try making this stitch with some woolen floss for a truly spectacular raised effect.

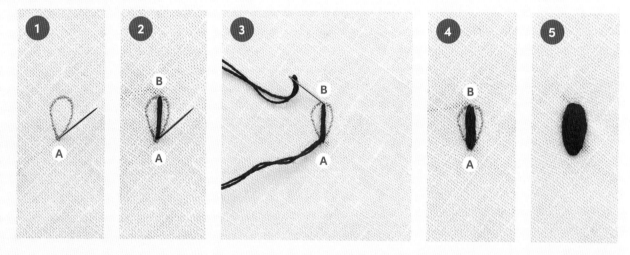

1. Bring the thread to the front of the fabric at A.

2. Take the needle to the back at B and pull through the fabric. Re-emerge at A, taking care to use exactly the same hole in the fabric.

3. Pull the thread through the fabric. Loop the thread to the left and take the needle to the back of the fabric at B. Gently pull the thread through, ensuring the stitch is positioned to the left of the first stitch.

4. Bring the thread to the front of the fabric at A and loop it to the right. Take the needle to the back at B. Gently pull the thread through, placing the stitch to the right of the previous stitches.

5. Work the required number of stitches (usually 7 to 10 would suffice), alternating them from the left side to the right side. After the last stitch, end on the back of the fabric.

FISHBONE STITCH

Difficulty Level: Easy

Used For: Leaves (especially ferns)

This "leaf stitch" is one of the most popular stitches to give a raised leaf effect; it is also surprisingly easy to master. The best part? Small mistakes don't spoil your stitch at all, because leaves in nature are never perfectly symmetrical!

TOP TIP: For an added texture, add some straight stitch "veins" in a lighter or darker shade along the center of your leaf embroidery.

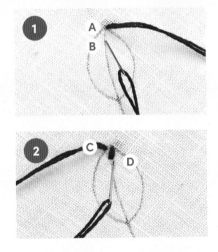

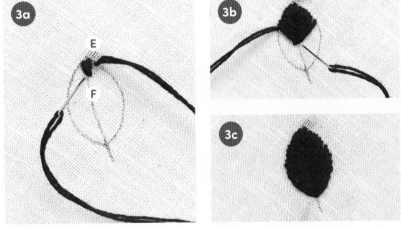

1. Bring the needle out of the fabric at A and make a small straight stitch to B, along the center line of the shape.

2. Next, bring the needle out of the fabric at C and make another straight stitch back to D, a little away from the center line of the shape.

3. Repeating in the other direction, bring the needle out of the fabric at E and make a stitch to F, overlapping the base of the previous stitch. This overlapping is a necessary feature of the fishbone stitch, and it is best achieved if you imagine two stitch lines parallel to the center line of the shape. (If you like, draw two such parallel lines with a pencil before starting your stitches.) So one stitch will rest on the border of the shape and then alternating stitches will rest on these imaginary stitch lines. It's these overlapping stitches that give this stitch its name, fishbone, as that's what it finally looks like!

BLANKET STITCH

Difficulty Level: Easy

Used For: Borders, outlines

In the olden days, this stitch was used to fasten two edges of a blanket together, hence the name! It is a beautiful stitch that works well as a border stitch or for embroidering floral shapes when used within a circular shape. Blanket stitch can be done as a straight line (Playing with Paisley, page 79) or as a half pinwheel (circle) or a full pinwheel; the full pinwheel is what we use to depict whimsical floral elements. I have included tutorials for both the straight blanket stitch as well as the pinwheel blanket stitch.

TOP TIP: Because the blanket stitch leaves space between stitches, improvise by filling up that space with French knots (in a straight blanket stitch) or straight stitches in a contrast color (in a pinwheel-shaped blanket stitch). This will add a lovely dimension to your design!

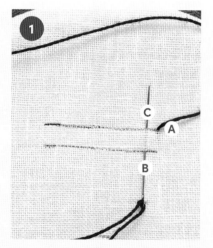

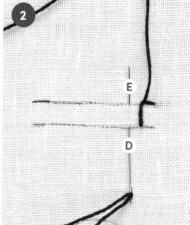

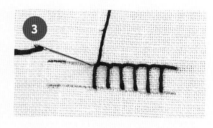

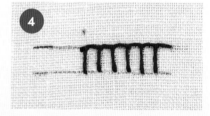

1. To make a simple blanket stitch, bring the thread to the front of the fabric at A. Take the needle to the back of the fabric at B and re-emerge at C at a right angle to both A and B. Ensure the thread is under the needle tip.

2. Pull the thread through the fabric until it lies snugly against the emerging thread but does not pull the fabric. Take the needle to the back at D and re-emerge at E, making sure that the thread lies under the tip of the needle.

3. Pull the thread through the fabric as before and keep making stitches in this fashion. To finish, take the needle to the back of the fabric just over the last loop.

4. Pull the thread through to the back of the fabric and secure it.

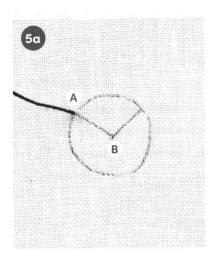

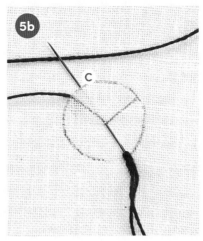

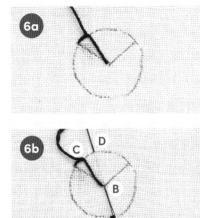

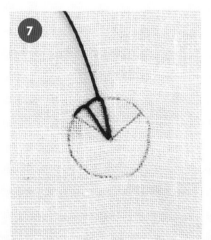

5. To embroider a pinwheel blanket stitch, mark the center of the template's circle. Bring the thread to the front of the fabric at A on the perimeter of the circle. Take the needle to the back of the fabric at the center of the circle at B. Re-emerge at C on the edge of the circle, about 1/16 inch (2 mm) from A. Make sure the thread is under the needle tip.

6. Pull the thread through the fabric until it lies snugly against the emerging thread but does not pull the fabric. Take the needle from B to D (which should be 1/16 inch [2 mm] from C).

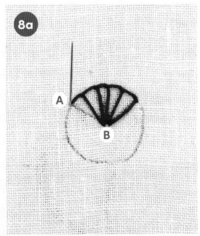

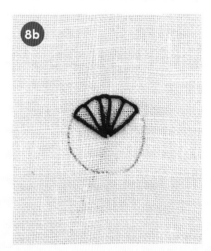

7. Keep making the stitches in this manner.

8. If you're embroidering a partial pinwheel: For the last stitch take the needle to the back of the fabric, where the pattern ends, just over the last loop. Re-emerge at A and proceed to take a straight stitch from A to B. Take the needle to the back of the fabric and secure the thread.

9. If you're embroidering a full pinwheel: For the last stitch, take the needle from the center of the circle to A. Pull the thread through the fabric as before and take the needle to the back just over the loop. Pull the thread through to the back of the fabric and secure it.

SOFT SHADING

Difficulty Level: Intermediate

Used For: Creating realistic elements (usually nature based)

Long and short stitch, or soft shading, forms the basis of all realistic embroidery styles. This is one stitch that you will get better at the more you practice, because the concept itself is very simple, but understanding the nuances of colors and positioning them takes practice. You will also get different results with different thicknesses and strands of floss. What you work with is up to your comfort level; however, it is good to note that this is a time-consuming stitch, even with multiple strands, so it is good to keep your patience levels high!

In the tutorial, I have used three rather distinct colors to highlight the stitches used; however, while soft shading, it is customary to use shades that are very close to each other so the blend is very natural.

TOP TIP: I recommend trying your hand first at soft shading with a thicker strand floss, like Pearl Cotton, until you are comfortable with the stitch; then you can move to a thinner strand floss like the DMC six-strand Mouliné range. Your margin of error will decrease with a thicker strand as it will fill up the space more quickly, even if the results won't be as fine as you will get with a thinner strand.

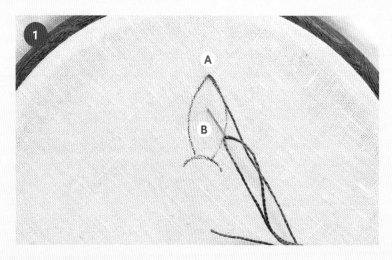

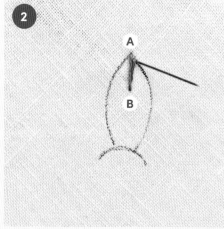

1. Bring the thread to the front of the fabric at A, on the outline. Take the needle to the back at B, inside the shape.

2. Pull the thread through the fabric. Re-emerge on the outline, very close to A. Pull the thread through again. Work a second stitch that is slightly shorter than the first stitch.

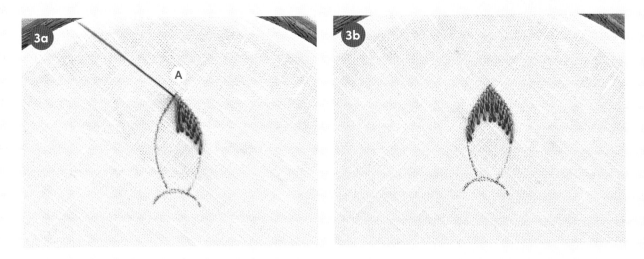

3. Continue working stitches very close together, fanning them to fit the shape. Alternate between long stitches and shorter stitches. Finish one half of the shape. Complete the other half in the same manner, then take the thread to the back of the fabric and end off.

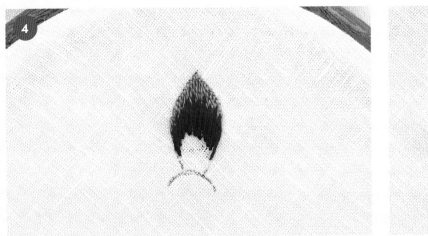

4. Using a darker shade of thread, bring the needle to the front of the fabric, splitting a stitch of the previous row. Pull the thread through. Take the needle to the back in the still-blank area. Work long and short stitches in the same direction as the first row (the long stitch in the first row will result in a long stitch in the second row and vice versa), always emerging through a previous stitch. When complete, end off as before.

OPTIONAL: Using an additionally darker shade of thread, bring the needle to the front of the fabric, repeating steps 3 and 4.

BRINGING IT TOGETHER
THE EMBROIDERY PROJECTS

Now we are entering the fun zone! I am so excited to share all the fun projects I have created for you, and I hope you are, too. Here is where we create beautiful embroidered designs, either as finished hoops, embroidered apparel or items of household use. The projects cover all fifteen stitches we have learned so far, and I have categorized them into three chapters, starting with six projects made entirely with single stitches. These will give you plenty of practice with these basic stitches and show you that even with a single stitch you can make something beautiful. The projects in the second chapter are a little more complex in that they use multiple stitches and the designs get more detailed and involved. The last chapter has seven projects for embroidering both apparel and homeware items. These will give you insight on how to use different kinds of pattern transfer methods and what special care needs to be taken, both while embroidering and for ongoing maintenance of these items. They are also larger projects, requiring more time to finish. It's a lesson in itself to persevere with an embroidery project that will take a few weeks to finish!

All twenty projects touch upon different design themes, so you can practice a variety of elements and decide for yourself what you love the most! The patterns range from floral designs, mandalas and geometric patterns to woodland creatures, fun animals, food items and landscapes. My favorites, of course, are the florals and the mandala!

Patterns, in my mind, serve merely as guidelines to implement your vision. They are meant to be modified, amended and added to. Take a project meant for a table runner and turn it into an embroidered hoop or vice versa. Once you are comfortable with the stitches, what you can do with these patterns is limited only by your imagination!

KEEP IT SIMPLE
SINGLE STITCH PATTERNS

The idea behind the single stitch projects in this chapter is to give you enough practice to master the stitch while at the same time making a lovely keepsake! They are centered on six of embroidery's basic stitches: running stitch, back stitch, stem stitch, chain stitch, satin stitch and French knots. It's my personal opinion that just about any embroidery project can be modified to be completed with one or more of these six stitches, so you'll definitely want to master them!

The projects here are listed in order from easiest to hardest, so you may wish to complete them in this order. To help with your practice, I have kept them very simple: The designs are straightforward (though they can be amended to add more stitches or elements), the color palettes are not too complex and each project is done with the same number of floss strands. I've also provided detailed instructions on how to go about embroidering each element of the designs. Because they all use a single stitch, I have focused on how to overcome some of the standard hurdles faced by crafters while working these stitches: navigating sharp corners, ending small or circular shapes and maintaining directionality. Honing these skills will help you tackle the multi-stitch projects you'll encounter in the later chapters.

Once you have mastered the original designs, you can take your skills to the next level by giving the design itself an upgrade or put it to an alternate use! For example, with Fishy Playdate (page 56)—my absolute favorite of these single stitch patterns—you can embroider it as an outline hoop, like I have done, or fill up the individual fish in colors of your choice, adding a few more basic stitches such as satin stitch and chain stitch. But don't limit yourself to just my suggestions—feel free to experiment with your own ideas!

OCEAN WAVES

Difficulty Level: Easy

Stitch Used: Running Stitch (page 26)

Are you ready to make your first embroidery project? As with every project in this chapter, this is made using only one stitch—in this case, the running stitch. This is a fun and easy project with which to ease into your embroidery journey.

For this pattern, we are using only three colors of floss. Feel free to alter the yellow or grey to a lighter or darker shade. However, I strongly recommend using variegated (shaded) floss for the waves; this helps give a three-dimensional effect without you having to worry about using different shades of a color in different waves. So you get this amazing shaded, shimmery effect without any extra effort on your part. To depict the sea's different moods, you can choose to use variegated green or grey instead of the shade of blue I have used.

MATERIALS

- Lightboard, to transfer the pattern (optional)
- Transfer pen (Frixion Heat Erasable Pen or any water-erasable pen)
- A minimum 8" (20-cm) square piece of white or off-white pure cotton or linen fabric
- 6" (15-cm) hoop with screws
- DMC 4025 (Caribbean Bay), 317 (Pewter Grey), 741 (Medium Tangerine)
- Size 3 embroidery needle
- Small embroidery scissors

The entire project is done with 6 strands of floss

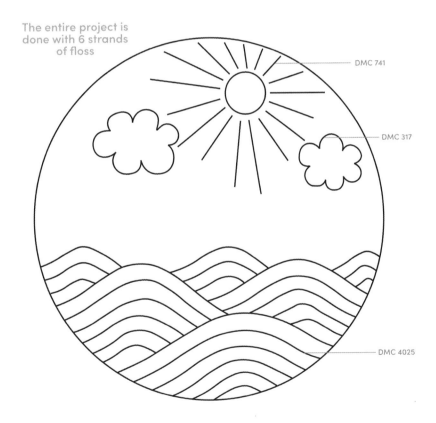

DMC 741

DMC 317

DMC 4025

1. Start by transferring the pattern and mounting the fabric on the hoop, making sure it's taut and the transferred pattern is centered (see "Getting Started," page 16).

2. To embroider the waves, start at any end of the hoop and use the running stitch with six strands of DMC 4025 to embroider all the layers of a single wave together. This will give the best 3D effect with the variegated floss. Make the stitches about 3 millimeters each and evenly spaced—take care not to stray from your pattern lines.

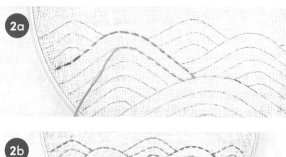

3. Next, embroider the clouds by starting from any of the curves of a cloud using six strands of DMC 317. Because these shapes have sharp edges pointing inward, you want to capture that through your embroidery. To do this, end the stitch for each curve right at the pointy edge. When you proceed to the next curve in the cloud, make the next stitch very near to the pointy edge to accentuate both the edge and the cloud.

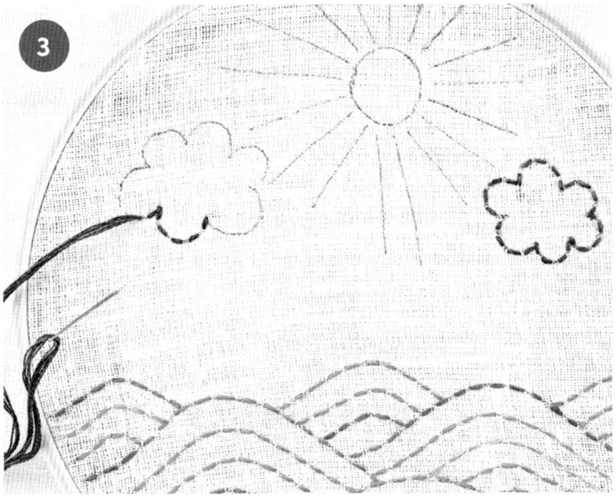

4. For the inner circle of the sun, take six strands of DMC 741 and make the stitches approximately 1⁄16 inch (2 mm) to highlight the curve. When you make the sun rays, after finishing one ray, take the floss behind the fabric and secure it at the back. DO NOT carry the floss forward to the next line, as it will show through the white fabric like a shadow. This is advice you want to follow for spaced-out elements whenever you are using light-colored fabrics.

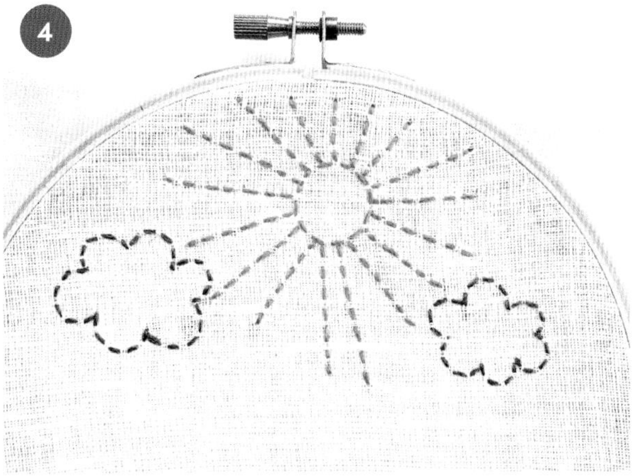

5. When you've finished embroidering the pattern, remove any stabilizer or pen marks. If needed, wash, dry and refix the embroidery in your hoop and then close and back your hoop (see page 22 for instructions).

FISHY PLAYDATE

Difficulty Level: Easy

Stitch Used: Back Stitch (page 27)

Fishy doodles are one of the first things kids learn to draw, so it's just natural for a fishy doodle embroidery design to be one of our first projects! This cute ode to childhood doodles is meant to help you navigate some of the trickier shapes to embroider with back stitch: how to turn a sharp corner so the crispness of the pattern is maintained through the embroidery, how to embroider small circular shapes, how to embroider curves and so forth.

There are five distinct fishes to model here; read through the instructions and, keeping the schematic handy, start with whichever fishy model you want to work with first!

MATERIALS

- Lightboard, to transfer the pattern (optional)
- Transfer pen (Frixion Heat Erasable Pen or any water-erasable pen)
- A minimum 8" (20-cm) square piece of light blue or light sea green cotton or linen fabric
- 6" (15-cm) hoop with screws
- DMC 806 (Dark Peacock Blue), 3041 (Medium Antique Violet), 961 (Dark Dusty Rose), 922 (Light Copper), 3799 (Very Dark Pewter Grey), 3827 (Pale Golden Brown), 3689 (Light Mauve), 166 (Lime Green), 743 (Medium Yellow)
- Size 5 embroidery needle
- Small embroidery scissors

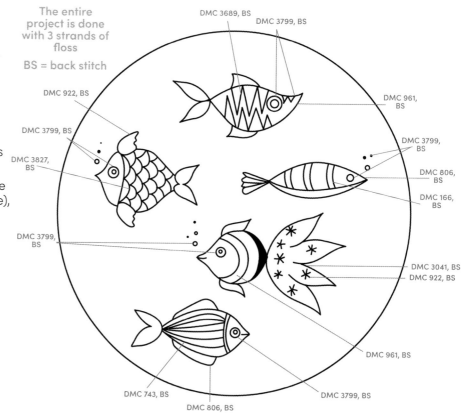

The entire project is done with 3 strands of floss

BS = back stitch

DMC 3689, BS
DMC 3799, BS
DMC 922, BS
DMC 961, BS
DMC 3799, BS
DMC 3799, BS
DMC 3827, BS
DMC 806, BS
DMC 166, BS
DMC 3799, BS
DMC 3041, BS
DMC 922, BS
DMC 961, BS
DMC 743, BS
DMC 806, BS
DMC 3799, BS

1. Start by transferring the pattern and mounting the fabric on the hoop (refer to "Getting Started" [page 16]), making sure it's taut and the transferred pattern is centered.

2. Begin embroidering the second right fish from the top using three strands of DMC 806 floss. When you come to a sharp corner, take the needle to the back of the fabric right at the corner—any time you turn a sharp corner, you want to make sure that the crispness of the pattern is maintained. Bring the needle out about 1/16 inch (2 mm) on the embroidery line that is at an angle and pull the thread through the fabric. Take the needle back to the pointy edge of the sharp corner, in the same hole where you first took it to the back of the fabric. Pull the thread through and continue stitching. Referring to the schematic, embroider the outlines of all the fishes using three strands of DMC 3041, DMC 806, DMC 961 and DMC 922.

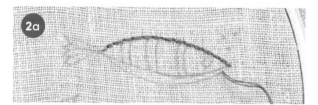

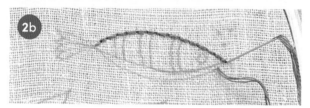

3. Back stitch is one of the best stitches to use when you have small circular elements like eyes to embroider. For all of the fishes, using three strands of DMC 3799, start at any point in the circle, making your stitches even smaller than usual, less than 1 millimeter. Always make sure you take the needle back into the same hole. Keeping these two points in mind is a surefire way of ensuring that the circular shape comes out well. For the last stitch, take the needle back into the hole where you emerged for the first stitch.

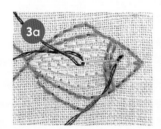

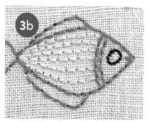

4. Next we will tackle how to embroider the different shapes inside the fish. To embroider shapes with curves, use three strands of DMC 3827 in the second to the left fish from the top; make smaller stitches than usual and make sure to take your needle back to the same hole as the previous stitch. Similarly, referring to the schematic, outline the inside of all the fishes using three strands of DMC 3689, DMC 166, DMC 961 and DMC 743.

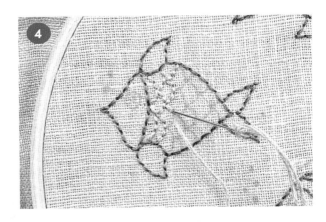

5. For two of the fish, we will be filling in some of the elements with back stitch. For the fish in the photo, using three strands of DMC 961, make small, even stitches close to one of the borders of the area you want to fill in. Staying true to the shape of the border, keep making consecutive back stitched lines. Once the entire area is filled up, take the needle to the back and secure the thread. We will be filling in another fish with DMC 166 using the same principle (refer to schematics).

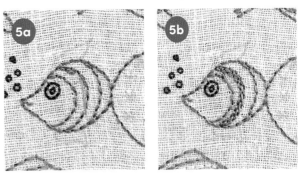

6. In this step, we'll use the straight stitch, which is a simple variant of back stitch. It is a single stitch taken between two points in any direction and of any length. In this pattern, we are embroidering a star shape using the straight stitch and three strands of DMC 922. Make a stitch from the center of the star shape to one of the spoke's ends. Take the needle to the back of the fabric and emerge again from the center of the shape, and make another stitch to another spoke. Continue making stitches until the entire star shape is completed.

7. When you've finished embroidering the pattern, remove any stabilizer or pen marks. If needed, wash, dry and refix the embroidery in your hoop and then close and back your hoop (see page 22 for instructions).

THE CHAKRA CHRONICLES

Difficulty Level: Easy

Stitch Used: Stem Stitch (page 28)

Mandalas are the most soothing patterns to embroider—not least because their repetitive nature helps create a calming rhythm. However, what I love the most about mandalas and why they're one of my favorite patterns to work on is how versatile they are! You can simply outline them for a minimalistic project or fill every bit of them with color. Either way, you'll end up with a finished piece that will stand out. Experiment with monochrome colors or all the shades of the rainbow. With a mandala pattern, you just can't go wrong! I have done this pattern as an outline with just the stem stitch, and I love how it makes the delicate curves of the petals shine. However, once you are comfortable with different stitches, experiment with filling in some portions of the pattern with satin stitch or herringbone stitch. I have done that modification and turned this beautiful mandala into the center embroidery in a cushion cover (page 6).

MATERIALS

- Lightboard, to transfer the pattern (optional)
- Transfer pen (Frixion Heat Erasable Pen or any water-erasable pen)
- A minimum 7" (18-cm) square piece of beige or ecru pure cotton or linen fabric
- 5" (13-cm) hoop with screws
- DMC 210 (Medium Lavender), 553 (Violet), 550 (Very Dark Violet), 4210 (Radiant Ruby), 166 (Lime Green), 3852 (Very Dark Straw), 413 (Dark Pewter Grey)
- Size 5 embroidery needle
- Small embroidery scissors

The entire project is done with 3 strands of floss

DMC 413, Stem Stitch

DMC 166, Stem Stitch

DMC 550, Stem Stitch

DMC 3852, Stem Stitch

DMC 550, Stem Stitch

DMC 210, Stem Stitch

DMC 4210, Stem Stitch

DMC 553, Stem Stitch

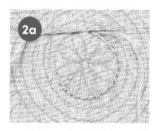

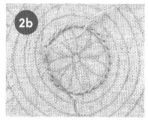

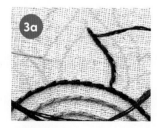

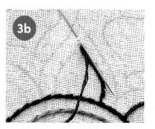

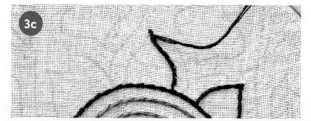

1. Start by transferring the pattern and mounting the fabric on the hoop (refer to "Getting Started" [page 16]), making sure it's taut and the transferred pattern is centered.

2. Begin embroidering the innermost of the concentric circles using three strands of DMC 210. This is an easy flowing shape and a good place to start practicing your stem stitch skills. Make stitches around 1/16 inch (2 mm) long, always making sure that the thread sits below the needle. In order to end the stitch seamlessly, when you are on your last stitch, take the needle through the center of the first stitch to the back of the fabric. Pull the thread through the fabric and end the stitch. Embroider the outer concentric circles in the same manner as per the schematic stitch guide, using three strands of DMC 553 and DMC 550 respectively.

3. Next we will learn how to embroider sharp corners, which most beginner embroiderers find difficult with the stem stitch. More often than not, they end up stitching in a way that turns the corner into a curve. Embroider the inner leaf shape using three strands of DMC 550, and when you come to a sharp corner in your pattern, stop short of the last stitch. Make a stitch from the edge of the corner, ensuring the thread is under the needle. Pull the floss—you have finished embroidering one half of your sharply curving shape.

4. Now, take a very small stitch (covering just a thread or two), still keeping the thread under the needle, very near to the sharp edge. Pull the floss—you will see the fabric thread showing through your stitch. Keeping the floss under the needle, take a stem stitch along the pattern line. You will have made a beautifully sharp stem stitch corner! Embroider the outer leaf shape using three strands of DMC 4210 and the standalone teardrop shapes using three strands of DMC 166 following the same principle. Embroider the inner flowers using three strands of DMC 3852.

⨂

5. When you've finished embroidering the pattern, remove any stabilizer or pen marks. If needed, wash, dry and refix the embroidery in your hoop and then close and back your hoop (see page 22 for instructions).

⨂

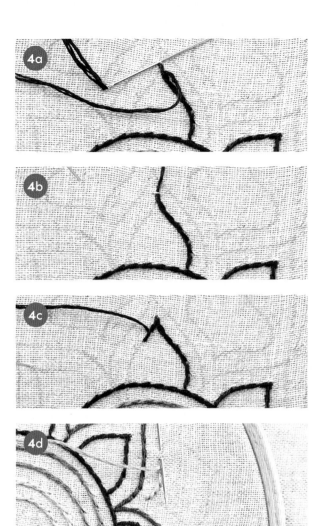

BLOOMING HEARTS

Difficulty Level: Easy

Stitch Used: Chain Stitch (page 31)

Chain stitch is my favorite stitch to play around with, and I would love for you to experiment with it, too—it lends itself so beautifully to creating borders as well as filling up spaces, and it looks so sophisticated! In this beginner project, we will use the chain stitch both to outline stitch and to fill up a small area. Because the entire project is done with only one stitch, we will focus on ways to navigate this stitch around tricky sharp corners and small circular elements (like an eye!). There is no fixed place to begin the project—you can start with whichever element strikes your fancy! I have started the project embroidering the central stem and followed up with the leaves, the heart element and the flowers. However, feel free to change up the order if you prefer—it will make no difference to your final result. And remember to have fun!

MATERIALS

- Lightboard, to transfer the pattern (optional)
- Transfer pen (Frixion Heat Erasable Pen or any water-erasable pen)
- A minimum 8" (20-cm) square piece of light green or soft pastel shade of cotton or linen fabric
- 6" (15-cm) hoop with screws
- DMC 3746 (Dark Blue Violet), 814 (Dark Garnet), 720 (Dark Orange Spice), 3804 (Dark Cyclamen Pink), 725 (Topaz), 3345 (Dark Hunter Green), 469 (Avocado Green)
- Size 5 embroidery needle
- Small embroidery scissors

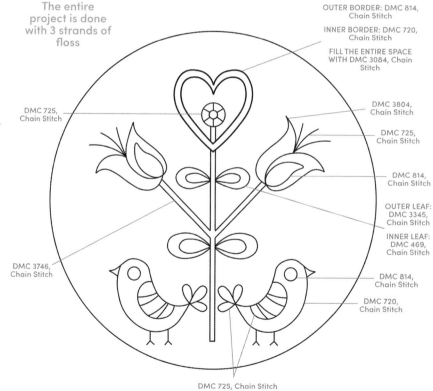

The entire project is done with 3 strands of floss

OUTER BORDER: DMC 814, Chain Stitch

INNER BORDER: DMC 720, Chain Stitch

FILL THE ENTIRE SPACE WITH DMC 3084, Chain Stitch

DMC 725, Chain Stitch

DMC 3804, Chain Stitch

DMC 725, Chain Stitch

DMC 814, Chain Stitch

OUTER LEAF: DMC 3345, Chain Stitch

INNER LEAF: DMC 469, Chain Stitch

DMC 814, Chain Stitch

DMC 3746, Chain Stitch

DMC 720, Chain Stitch

DMC 725, Chain Stitch

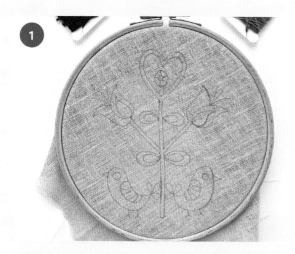

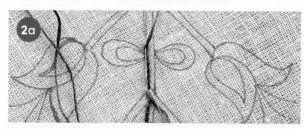

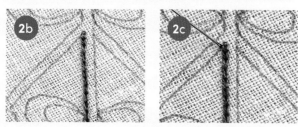

1. Start by transferring the pattern and mounting the fabric on the hoop (refer to "Getting Started" [page 16]), making sure it's taut and the transferred pattern is centered.

❧

2. Start the project by embroidering the central stem with three strands of DMC 3746. Make neat and even stitches not more than 2 to 3 millimeters in length until you reach the first sharp corner. Take the thread to the back of the fabric (as if you are closing the stitch) and bring it out on the line at an angle, very close to the stitch, roughly a thread or two away.

❧

3. Turn the hoop around and make a chain stitch. Continue stitching.

❧

4. Next we will navigate curves, especially small ones like the bird's eye. Take three strands of DMC 814 and keep the stitches even smaller than usual—around 1 millimeter. This will ensure that the curved shape emerges beautifully. To finish the circle seamlessly, work the last stitch, then take the needle to the back of the fabric and emerge from inside (within) the first stitch. Pull the thread through the fabric, remembering to loop it around the needle. Complete the stitch. Embroider the rest of the curved shapes following the same principle with the help of the schematics using three strands of DMC 720, DMC 3804, DMC 725, DMC 3345 and DMC 469.

❧

5. Next we fill in the heart motif with the chain stitch. Outline the outer and inner borders of the heart with DMC 814 and DMC 720. This will leave a little empty space between the borders. Fill in with another line of chain stitch embroidered with DMC 3804. Because the area is already marked by the two outer borders, this is a fun way to fill up a space. Some fabric will likely show through the stitches in certain places, but that will only add to the beauty of your handmade piece.

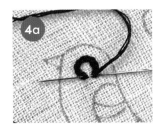
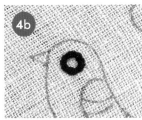

≫

6. Last, embroider the bird's legs using three strands of DMC 720 and a detached chain stitch, which is an interesting variant of the chain stitch. Can you guess what it is? You guessed right! This is a standalone single chain stitch you make in a pattern. In this pattern, to embroider the forked legs of the birdie, you need to make a couple of chain stitches to cover the main portion of the leg and then take two detached (single) chain stitches in forked directions for the claws. Cute, isn't it?

≫

7. When you've finished embroidering the pattern, remove any stabilizer or pen marks. If needed, wash, dry and refix the embroidery in your hoop and then close and back your hoop (see page 22 for instructions).

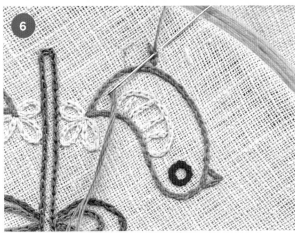

≫

FALLING FOR FEATHERS

Difficulty Level: Easy

Stitch Used: Satin Stitch (page 29)

Satin stitch lends itself well to almost all designs—it's so versatile! So why a feather, you may ask? Because the natural texture of a feather is a little uneven, with ridges on the outer edges. So when you are embroidering satin stitch with little or no practice, your edges may not be as smooth as you would like. But with a feather pattern, it won't look ungainly! If anything, it will look very natural and add to the uniqueness of your embroidered piece, while giving you practice with the stitch.

MATERIALS

- Lightboard, to transfer the pattern (optional)
- Transfer pen (Frixion Heat Erasable Pen, or any water-erasable pen)
- A minimum 8" (20-cm) square piece of beige or cream pure cotton or linen fabric
- 6" (15-cm) hoop with screws
- DMC 543 (Very Light Beige Brown), 783 (Medium Topaz), 919 (Red Copper), 779 (Brown), 924 (Very Dark Grey Green), 738 (Very Light Tan), 3815 (Dark Celadon Green), 993 (Very Light Aquamarine), 961 (Dark Dusty Rose), 3727 (Light Antique Mauve), 451 (Dark Shell Grey)
- Size 5 embroidery needle
- Small embroidery scissors

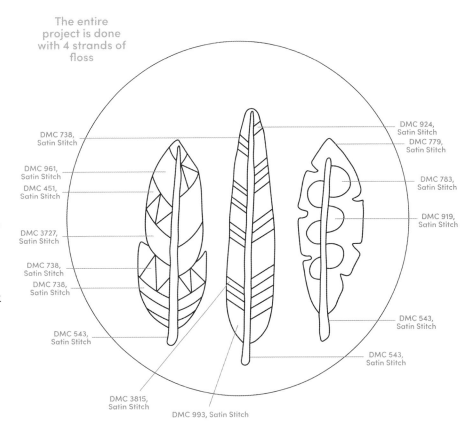

The entire project is done with 4 strands of floss

DMC 738, Satin Stitch

DMC 961, Satin Stitch

DMC 451, Satin Stitch

DMC 3727, Satin Stitch

DMC 738, Satin Stitch

DMC 738, Satin Stitch

DMC 543, Satin Stitch

DMC 3815, Satin Stitch

DMC 993, Satin Stitch

DMC 924, Satin Stitch

DMC 779, Satin Stitch

DMC 783, Satin Stitch

DMC 919, Satin Stitch

DMC 543, Satin Stitch

DMC 543, Satin Stitch

1. Start by transferring the pattern and mounting the fabric on the hoop (refer to "Getting Started" [page 16]), making sure it's taut and the transferred pattern is centered.

2. Embroider the central shaft of all the three feathers with four strands of DMC 543. Next, embroider the rightmost feather, beginning with the inner half circles using four strands of DMC 783 and DMC 919, as per the schematic. For a circular shape, you should always start the stitches in the middle of the shape, finish one half of the shape and then embroider the second half. This will ensure that the stitches lay perpendicular to the shape and look even.

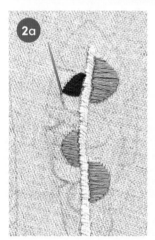
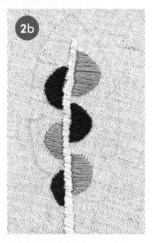

3. To finish the rightmost feather, embroider the outer feather strands with four strands of DMC 779. With satin stitch, it is very important to maintain the directionality of your stitches—that will go a long way in giving the right textural feel to your element! In a feather, for instance, you want your stitches to go perpendicular to the feather axis just as it would on an actual feather. To embroider the outer area of the feather, I highly recommend drawing "reference" lines along the wave of the pattern with your Frixion pen to help you stay in the right direction. I do this even today, with many years of embroidery experience behind me. I find doing this keeps the embroidery simple and you avoid having to unravel your stitches because your stitches were not aligned!

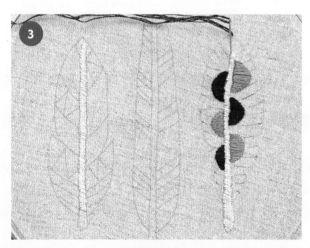

4. Another challenge is navigating irregular shapes, for example the outer area of this feather. Because the inner border is smaller than the outer border, you might end up stitching "over," which will give a bunching effect. But on a feather, you want a satiny effect. What I do in such designs is make a few stitches a little shorter on the inner side than their neighbors, while keeping the stitches on the outer edges adjacent to each other; this will give you extra surface to work your stitches, while not overlapping them! The finished feather should look just slightly raised without any unevenness.

❧

5. Next, embroider the middle feather, making your stitches as per the schematic using four strands of DMC 924, DMC 738, DMC 3815 and DMC 993, making sure each of the stitches is along the stitch line. You want all the stitched blocks to be parallel to each other.

❧

6. Last, make the leftmost feather, embroidering the non-triangular shapes in the same manner as step 5, using four strands of DMC 961, DMC 3727 and DMC 738, referring to the schematic for exact placement. For making the triangular shapes, take four strands of DMC 451 and DMC 783, and always start embroidering from a wide base of the triangle and toward the pointier edges. Because you are stitching a feather and you want it to look realistic, stitch all the triangular shapes perpendicular to the quill/shaft of the feather.

❧

7. When you've finished embroidering the pattern, remove any stabilizer or pen marks. If needed, wash, dry and refix the embroidery in your hoop and then close and back your hoop (see page 22 for instructions).

❧

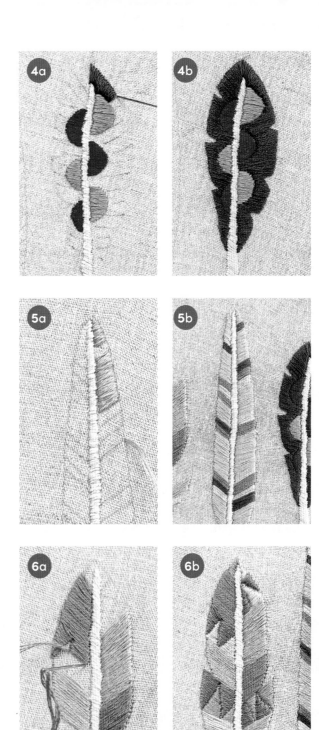

SPRINKLES ON MY DONUT

Difficulty Level: Intermediate

Stitch Used: French Knots (page 32)

This is an adorable pattern, easy to understand and execute. But make no mistake, French knots take time—so keep an extra portion of patience handy for this one and you won't be disappointed with the amazing textures in your finished project! I totally recommend you use this pattern on the back of a toddler's jacket or on a bag . . . it would look so beautiful!

A very useful tip for embroidering French knots is to use even-numbered floss strands and fold them over (that is, for the four strands we are using in this project, take two strands and fold them over). That way the number of strands you are pulling through along with the needle will never exceed the total number of strands you are using. This will ensure less floss thickness along the eye of the needle when you're making your knots, reducing the chance of creating tangles.

MATERIALS

- Lightboard, to transfer the pattern (optional)
- Transfer pen (Frixion Heat Erasable Pen or any water-erasable pen)
- A minimum 7" (18-cm) square piece of white pure cotton or linen fabric
- 5" (13-cm) hoop with screws
- DMC 938 (Ultra Dark Coffee Brown), 581 (Moss Green), 3844 (Dark Bright Turquoise), 3340 (Medium Apricot), 3607 (Light Plum), 553 (Violet), 742 (Light Tangerine), 747 (Very Light Sky Blue), 353 (Peach), 3689 (Light Mauve), 211 (Light Lavender), 745 (Light Pale Yellow), 369 (Very Light Pistachio Green)
- Size 3 embroidery needle
- Small embroidery scissors

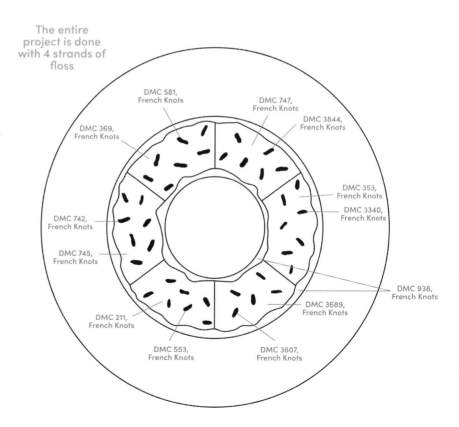

The entire project is done with 4 strands of floss

DMC 581, French Knots

DMC 747, French Knots

DMC 3844, French Knots

DMC 369, French Knots

DMC 353, French Knots

DMC 3340, French Knots

DMC 742, French Knots

DMC 745, French Knots

DMC 938, French Knots

DMC 211, French Knots

DMC 3689, French Knots

DMC 553, French Knots

DMC 3607, French Knots

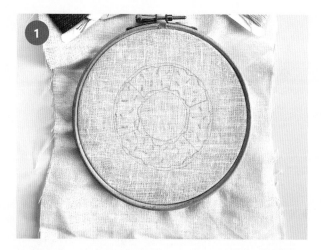

1. Start by transferring the pattern and mounting the fabric on the hoop (refer to "Getting Started" [page 16]), making sure it's taut and the transferred pattern is centered.

2. Begin sewing by embroidering the outlines, from any point on the outer border, using four strands of DMC 938 to ensure that you have the shape right. This is a good tip to keep in mind when filling in any shape with French knots. To ensure that you keep to the stitch line, bring your needle out one thread inside the stitch line and take it back on the stitch line when completing the French knot. Complete the entire outside and inside circular outlines in this manner.

3. Next, embroider the inner borders (the squiggly ones), again with DMC 938. At this stage, do not worry about filling in the empty spaces in between. Once both the inner outlines are made, proceed to fill in the empty spaces with more French knots until the entire area is filled in.

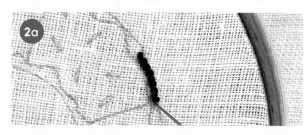

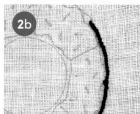
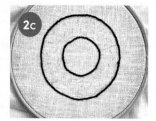

4. Once the "chocolate icing" portion of the donut is embroidered, move to embroidering the "sprinkles" as per the schematic. We will use four strands of DMC 581, DMC 3844, DMC 3340, DMC 3607, DMC 553 and DMC 742—you can either place them as per the schematic or make your own fun placements! Complete all six sections. Isn't it already looking so much like a donut?

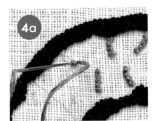 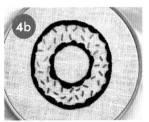

❧

5. For the final portion of this project, we will fill in each of the sections using the lighter floss shades (DMC 747, DMC 353, DMC 3689, DMC 211, DMC 745 and DMC 369). Again, the first step is to outline the shape you are planning to fill in. Because these shapes are irregular and won't always have a stitch line for you to follow, make your stitches close to the embroidered border you are making your outline against. Once a section is outlined, you can proceed to fill it up. Complete all the sections in this manner.

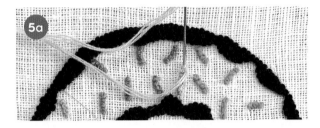

❧

6. When you've finished embroidering the pattern, remove any stabilizer or pen marks. If needed, wash, dry and refix the embroidery in your hoop and then close and back your hoop (see page 22 for instructions).

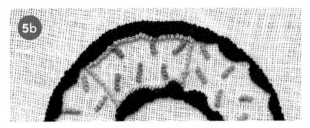

❧

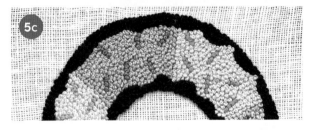

MORE STITCHES, MORE FUN
MULTI-STITCH PATTERNS

You have learned the stitches and made some single stitch projects! Are you ready to take your embroidery skills to the next level? In this section, we will practice embroidering with different numbers of strands for different elements, more floss colors and a wider variety of stitches. Keep the schematic charts handy when embroidering projects from here on. Schematics will end up being your best friend, making it easy for you to know at a quick glance which stitch and floss number and how many strands to use. The patterns from now on will take longer to finish, but finishing them will also make you so proud of yourself—and rightly so!

The designs covered in this section are selected to help you understand a variety of techniques. You'll learn how a project looks when filled entirely with just satin stitch, like in The Blue Door of My Dreams (page 87), versus back stitch *and* satin stitch, like in Kitty on My Books (page 82), so you can decide which method you prefer for future projects. You'll also learn how to embroider letters in the "Life Is Beautiful" Wreath (page 92) and Pretty in Pastel Rainbow (page 107). This is a useful skill when you want to personalize projects later on. With the Welcoming Spring Flower Bouquet (page 97), we'll go all out using bright colors while we embroider using only pastels in Pretty in Pastel Rainbow (page 107). Each theme here will help you get the hang of embroidering different elements. Eventually, you will decide for yourself which particular elements you enjoy embroidering the most!

PLAYING WITH PAISLEY

Difficulty Level: Intermediate

Stitches Used: Stem Stitch (page 28), Blanket Stitch (page 44), French Knots (page 32), Herringbone Stitch (page 37), Back Stitch (page 27), Satin Stitch (page 29), Chain Stitch (page 31)

Paisleys are one of my favorite folk-inspired motifs to work with! They are so versatile, and you can add to or modify the pattern with just some simple tweaks. The first of the multi-stitch projects, this is more or less a sampler of almost all the basic stitches. I have put the difficulty level as intermediate because this is the first project where we will use different numbers of strands for different elements. I have designed the color scheme of this pattern to resemble a peacock feather, and I hope you think it looks as beautiful as I do!

MATERIALS

- Lightboard, to transfer the pattern (optional)
- Transfer pen (Frixion Heat Erasable Pen or any water-erasable pen)
- A minimum 7" (18-cm) square piece of white or soft-colored pure cotton or linen fabric
- 5" (13-cm) hoop with screws
- DMC 550 (Very Dark Violet), 3812 (Very Dark Seagreen), 972 (Deep Canary), 3845 (Medium Bright Turquoise), 995 (Dark Electric Blue), 820 (Very Dark Royal Blue), 166 (Lime Green), 469 (Avocado Green)
- Size 3 and 5 embroidery needles (size 3 for French knots and size 5 for the rest of the stitches)
- Small embroidery scissors

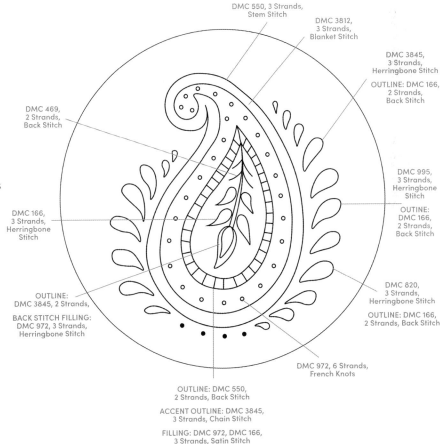

DMC 550, 3 Strands, Stem Stitch

DMC 3812, 3 Strands, Blanket Stitch

DMC 3845, 3 Strands, Herringbone Stitch

OUTLINE: DMC 166, 2 Strands, Back Stitch

DMC 469, 2 Strands, Back Stitch

DMC 995, 3 Strands, Herringbone Stitch

OUTLINE: DMC 166, 2 Strands, Back Stitch

DMC 166, 3 Strands, Herringbone Stitch

DMC 820, 3 Strands, Herringbone Stitch

OUTLINE: DMC 166, 2 Strands, Back Stitch

OUTLINE: DMC 3845, 2 Strands,

BACK STITCH FILLING: DMC 972, 3 Strands, Herringbone Stitch

DMC 972, 6 Strands, French Knots

OUTLINE: DMC 550, 2 Strands, Back Stitch

ACCENT OUTLINE: DMC 3845, 3 Strands, Chain Stitch

FILLING: DMC 972, DMC 166, 3 Strands, Satin Stitch

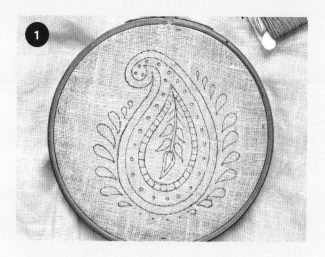

1. Start by transferring the pattern and mounting the fabric on the hoop (refer to "Getting Started" [page 16]), making sure it's taut and the transferred pattern is centered.

≈

2. Begin embroidering the outline of the paisley with stem stitch using three strands of DMC 550, making sure the floss is always below the needle. Next, embroider the inner border with blanket stitch using three strands of DMC 3812. While making blanket stitch, always keep the stitches the same size and the needle perpendicular to the stitch line. You want to be careful not to pull the floss too much nor keep it too loose.

≈

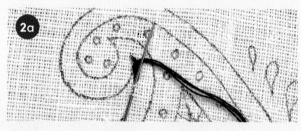

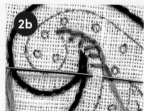

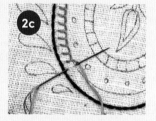

3. Next, tackle the French knots, taking three strands of DMC 972 and doubling them over. If you want your French knots to look bigger, wrap the thread twice around the needle instead of just once.

≈

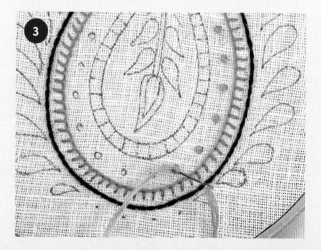

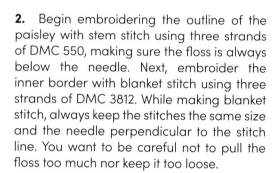

4. Next, embroider the outer teardrop shapes with herringbone stitch using three strands of DMC 3845, DMC 995 and DMC 820 (refer to the schematic for exact placement). I really like the finish the herringbone stitch gives the curved teardrop shape.

✎

5. To emphasize the curvature of the shape even more, outline it with back stitch using two strands of DMC 166, keeping the stitches small and even. Take the back stitches through the same stitch holes as your earlier herringbone stitches. Finish outlining all the teardrop shapes.

✎

6. Next, outline the inner paisley border with back stitch using two strands of DMC 550. Make the inner boxes using straight/single back stitches. Fill in the shapes alternately with three strands of DMC 972 and DMC 166 using satin stitch.

✎

7. Outline the inner paisley with chain stitch using three strands of DMC 3845, keeping your stitches right next to the back stitch border you already embroidered. Making two borders accentuates the design—it's also a lovely way to fill up the space using line stitches. Embroider the inner stem using two strands of DMC 469 with back stitch and leaves using herringbone stitch with three strands of DMC 166, referring to the schematic. Embroider the central bud with three strands of DMC 972 using herringbone stitch and outline using two strands of DMC 3845 with back stitch.

✎

8. When you've finished, remove any stabilizer or pen marks. If needed, wash, dry and refix the embroidery in your hoop and then close and back your hoop (see page 22 for instructions).

✎

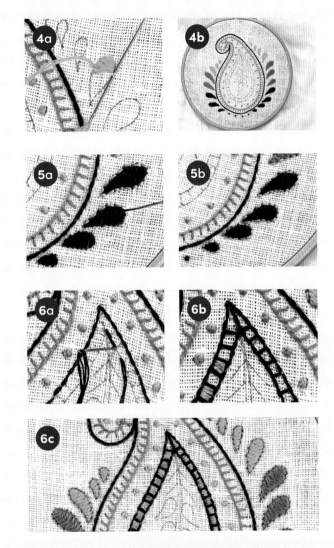

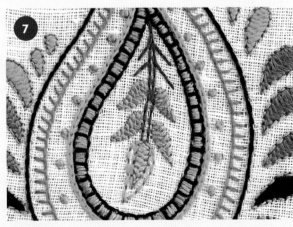

KITTY ON MY BOOKS

Difficulty Level: Intermediate

Stitches Used: Satin Stitch (page 29), Back Stitch (page 27), Long and Short Stitch (or Soft Shading; page 46)

How cute are cats? And I absolutely love embroidering books in perspective—they take time, but they come out looking so sophisticated! This is the first of two projects that we will "fill up" using different stitches.

Filling up spaces takes up a lot of stitches and can sometimes pull or pucker your fabric, so when attempting these projects, I recommend using two layers of fabric to give it durability. Note how I have used the fabric color as the wall background—that is an excellent way of showing a "colored" wall/background frame without actually embroidering it all. Choose a color of your choice—blue, grey, green or purple—they'll all go with this color scheme.

MATERIALS

- Lightboard, to transfer the pattern (optional)
- Transfer pen (Frixion Heat Erasable Pen or any water-erasable pen)
- 2 minimum 7" (18-cm) square pieces of burnt orange (or any color) pure cotton or linen fabric
- 5" (13-cm) hoop with screws
- DMC 813 (Light Blue), 745 (Light Pale Yellow), 3750 (Very Dark Antique Blue), 310 (Black), 520 (Dark Fern Green), 3041 (Medium Antique Violet), 610 (Dark Drab Brown), 524 (Very Light Fern Green), 154 (Very Dark Red), 4503 (Wisteria), 169 (Pewter Grey)
- Size 5 embroidery needle
- Small embroidery scissors

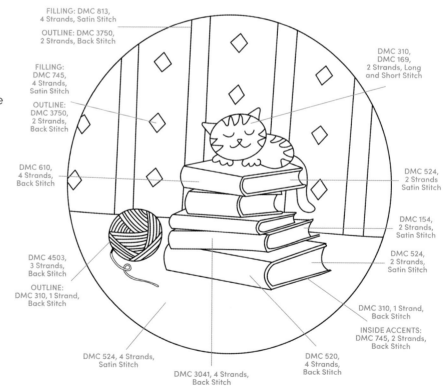

FILLING: DMC 813, 4 Strands, Satin Stitch

OUTLINE: DMC 3750, 2 Strands, Back Stitch

FILLING: DMC 745, 4 Strands, Satin Stitch

OUTLINE: DMC 3750, 2 Strands, Back Stitch

DMC 610, 4 Strands, Back Stitch

DMC 4503, 3 Strands, Back Stitch

OUTLINE: DMC 310, 1 Strand, Back Stitch

DMC 310, DMC 169, 2 Strands, Long and Short Stitch

DMC 524, 2 Strands, Satin Stitch

DMC 154, 2 Strands, Satin Stitch

DMC 524, 2 Strands, Satin Stitch

DMC 310, 1 Strand, Back Stitch

INSIDE ACCENTS: DMC 745, 2 Strands, Back Stitch

DMC 524, 4 Strands, Satin Stitch

DMC 3041, 4 Strands, Back Stitch

DMC 520, 4 Strands, Back Stitch

1. Start by transferring the pattern and mounting the fabric on the hoop (refer to "Getting Started" [page 16]), making sure it's taut and the transferred pattern is centered.

∽

2. Embroider the wall panels using four strands of DMC 813 with satin stitch, taking near horizontal stitches, bearing in mind that filling so many panels with satin stitch will take a little time. Embroider the little diamond pattern with satin stitch as well, using four strands of DMC 745, but this time taking a vertical stitch down the center of the diamond and then embroidering both sides with satin stitch. Highlight the entire "wall" with a border of back stitch using two strands of DMC 3750. This will hide any little mistakes that might have occurred in the length of the satin stitch.

∽

3. Next, outline the books with just one strand of DMC 310 using back stitch. When you fill up a space using back stitch, it tends to "overfill" the portion you are embroidering—so I always advise making an outline before *and* after using the filling stitch, but with a single strand of floss. Just using one strand for our outline will ensure that it doesn't overpower the embroidery itself. If you are filling a space with satin stitch, just one outline done *after* the filling stitch will be enough (as we did in the wall panel).

∽

4. Next, fill in the space within the books with neat and small back stitches using four strands of DMC 520, DMC 3041 and DMC 610. Fill only the sides and fronts with back stitch. For the "pages," make long satin stitches spanning the entire length with two strands of DMC 524 and DMC 154, which will look like pages of a book. Now that you have filled up the books, finish it off with another round of outlining with one strand of DMC 310. The finished structure will look sharp and beautifully three-dimensional.

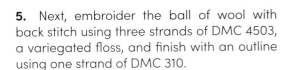

5. Next, embroider the ball of wool with back stitch using three strands of DMC 4503, a variegated floss, and finish with an outline using one strand of DMC 310.

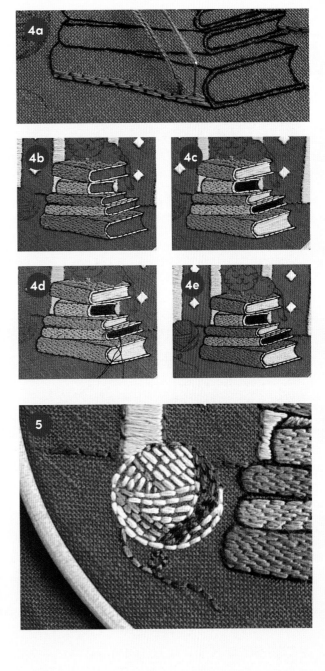

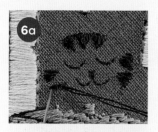

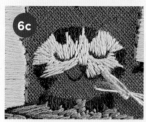

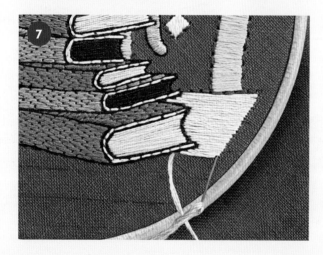

6. Let's move on to something that scares a lot of folks—soft shading. Because the final effect is so beautiful, everyone assumes this stitch will be difficult! But that is not the case, because we will go about embroidering it methodically. Embroider the black accents (stripes) of the cat with two strands of DMC 310 using satin stitch (vertical stitches). Now take alternate long and short stitches with two strands of DMC 169 to fill in. You want to take your stitches around the eyes, nose and mouth—the whole effect will be circular, just how fur would grow on a cat's face! Draw reference lines with your Frixion pen if needed to help you keep the direction, like I have done for the cat's lower body. Don't worry if, at the midway stage, it doesn't look as good as you expect it to—once finished, it will look just perfect. Finish by outlining the entire cat with one strand of DMC 310.

7. Draw reference lines for the tabletop/floor to help you keep your long satin stitches straight. Using four strands of DMC 524, take stitches to fill up the entire bottom half of the hoop; if the stitches span the length of the hoop, then that is also OK! Once finished, your floor will give a lovely contrast/backdrop for your books and wall panel to shine against.

8. When you've finished embroidering the pattern, remove any stabilizer or pen marks. If needed, wash, dry and refix the embroidery in your hoop and then close and back your hoop (see page 22 for instructions).

THE BLUE DOOR OF MY DREAMS

Difficulty Level: Intermediate

Stitches Used: Satin Stitch (page 29), Back Stitch (page 27), Stem Stitch Rose (page 40)

Making an embroidery design almost entirely with satin stitch looks gorgeous texturally—but it also requires a lot of patience and time. That is why, even though the stitches involved are quite easy, I have put the difficulty level of this project as intermediate. I have included this architectural design among all the floral ones because the margin for error here is smaller than you'd have in a flower or a leaf. But with a little patience and ensuring that you keep your satin along your stitch line, you will be sure to get a wonderful result! What's more, making your back stitch outlines *after* you have made your satin stitch embroidery will help cover those little irregularities in your stitches. I always recommend making outlines in an architectural project after the satin stitch is done.

MATERIALS

- Lightboard, to transfer the pattern (optional)
- Transfer pen (Frixion Heat Erasable Pen or any water-erasable pen)
- A minimum 7" (18-cm) square piece of beige pure cotton or linen fabric
- 5" (13-cm) hoop with screws
- DMC 807 (Peacock Blue), 972 (Deep Canary), 869 (Very Dark Hazelnut Brown), 422 (Light Hazelnut Brown), 318 (Light Steel Grey), 779 (Brown), 600 (Very Dark Cranberry), 3608 (Very Light Plum), 581 (Moss Green), 310 (Black)
- Size 5 embroidery needle
- Small embroidery scissors

The entire doorframe outline is done with DMC 310, 2 Strands, Back Stitch

DMC 972, 4 Strands, Satin Stitch

DMC 807, 4 Strands, Satin Stitch

DMC 869, 4 Strands, Satin Stitch

DMC 422, 4 Strands, Satin Stitch

Use the following colors randomly across all the flowers: DMC 600, DMC 3608, 4 Strands, Stem Stitch Rose

DMC 972, 4 Strands, Satin Stitch

DMC 581, 4 Strands, Satin Stitch

DMC 779, 4 Strands, Back Stitch

DMC 318, 4 Strands, Satin Stitch

DMC 422, 4 Strands Satin Stitch

DMC 807, 4 Strands, Satin Stitch

DMC 807, 4 Strands, Satin Stitch

DMC 869, 4 Strands, Satin Stitch

1. Start by transferring the pattern and mounting the fabric on the hoop (refer to "Getting Started" [page 16]), making sure it's taut and the transferred pattern is centered.

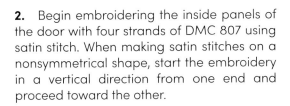

∞

2. Begin embroidering the inside panels of the door with four strands of DMC 807 using satin stitch. When making satin stitches on a nonsymmetrical shape, start the embroidery in a vertical direction from one end and proceed toward the other.

∞

3. Next, take four strands of DMC 972 and embroider the little yellow hearts using satin stitch *before* embroidering the corresponding door panel. Embroidering the hearts first will ensure that you are able to capture the shape perfectly, and then you can embroider the door panel around the hearts. For the bottom-most panel, make your satin stitches in the horizontal direction. This directional diversity is a great way to give a 3D effect to satin stitch embroidery.

∞

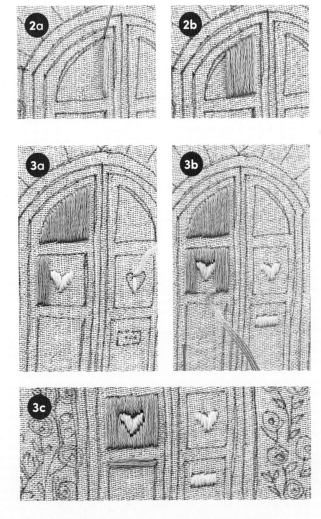

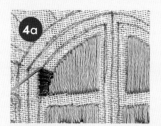

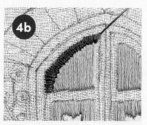

4. Next, embroider the doorframe imme-diately next to the panel with four strands of DMC 869 using satin stitches made horizontally. When embroidering layers of satin stitches next to each other, never skip a layer in between as that will distort your stitch lines. When you have to turn the corner, you need to take multiple stitches that end in the same stitch hole, until the stitches are parallel again. Embroider the frame next to it with four strands of DMC 807 and the outermost frame with four strands of DMC 422 (all with satin stitch).

5. Make the arched frame above the door alternately with four strands of DMC 422 and DMC 869 using satin stitch. Continuing to use satin stitch, embroider the diamond-shaped tile in the center with four strands of DMC 972 for the border and four strands of DMC 807 for the center.

6. Embroider the steps next, using four strands of DMC 318 with satin stitch. They have a 3D perspective to them, and to embroider them easily, we need to be a little clever. I always make lines with my Frixion pen highlighting how I want my stitches to proceed and that helps me get the perspec-tive just right.

7. Embroider the stems of the bushes on either side with four strands of DMC 779 using back stitch. Next, embroider the roses in two shades (four strands of DMC 600 and DMC 3608) using stem stitch rose. You can choose to place the lighter and the darker roses differently from me if you like! Finish it all with leaves embroidered with four strands of DMC 581 using satin stitch, which are just three straight stitches taken very close to each other, the ones on the side a little smaller than the center one. Unlike the standard satin stitches that are parallel, these will all end in the same stitch hole near the stem.

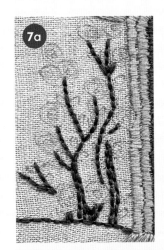

≈

8. Now that all the satin stitches are made, we move to the fun part! Make the outlines using two strands of DMC 310 with back stitch across the entire doorframe. Keep your stitches small and along the stitch lines of the satin stitches you made earlier—this will help you capture the straight lines you wish to highlight, and you will have a beautiful embroidered doorframe to show off!

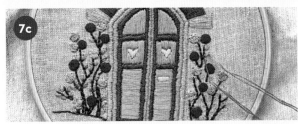

≈

9. When you've finished embroidering the pattern, remove any stabilizer or pen marks. If needed, wash, dry and refix the embroidery in your hoop and then close and back your hoop (see page 22 for instructions).

≈

"LIFE IS BEAUTIFUL" WREATH

Difficulty Level: Easy

Stitches Used: Stem Stitch (page 28), Satin Stitch (page 29), Back Stitch (page 27), French Knots (page 32), Woven Wheel Rose (page 38)

For this project, I have deliberately used a dark-colored fabric so I can highlight some benefits of tracing your pattern using a chalk pencil. (I use a Bohin retractable chalk pencil. A regular white chalk pencil or a white water-erasable pen will also do the job well.) Unlike a blue/black water soluble/heat drying pen, the design lines made by a chalk pencil tend to get lighter with time (they won't completely disappear, just get lighter), so you may need to redraw some elements of your pattern from time to time while embroidering. This reason is also why I tend to embroider the main design elements first (in this case, the intertwining stems and the skeleton of the woven wheel flowers) when I embroider on a darker fabric.

Coming to the design itself, you can embroider it alone or with the lettering. It's a beautiful minimalistic pattern that will pop out against the dark background of the fabric. The woven wheel roses and the French knots on the stems give it a lovely textural depth.

MATERIALS

- Lightboard, to transfer the pattern (optional)
- Transfer pen (white chalk pencil or white water-erasable pen)
- A minimum 7" (18-cm) square piece of dark grey pure cotton or linen fabric
- 6" (15-cm) hoop with screws
- DMC 522 (Fern Green), 3782 (Light Mocha Brown), 3803 (Dark Mauve), 3815 (Dark Celadon Green), 833 (Light Golden Olive), 3842 (Dark Wedgewood), 3688 (Medium Mauve), 4150 (Maple), 813 (Light Blue),
- Size 5 embroidery needle
- Small embroidery scissors

DMC 3815, 4 Strands Satin Stitch

DMC 522, 4 Strands, Stem Stitch

DMC 3782, 4 Strands, Stem Stitch

STEM: DMC 833, 4 Strands, Back Stitch

BERRIES: DMC 3842, 6 Strands, French Knots

DMC 3803, DMC 3688, 4 Strands, Woven Wheel Rose Stitch

DMC 4150, 6 Strands, Back Stitch

DMC 813, 4 Strands, Straight Stitch (Variant of Back Stitch)

CENTERS: DMC 833, 4 Strands, French Knots

1. Start by transferring the pattern and mounting the fabric on the hoop (refer to "Getting Started" [page 16]), making sure it's taut and the transferred pattern is centered.

2. Begin by embroidering both of the vines with stem stitch using three strands of DMC 522 and DMC 3782 floss. Becuase we are working with a dark fabric marked with a white chalk pencil, simultaneously embroider the spokes of the woven wheel flowers with four strands of DMC 3803 using straight stitches so as to mark their place.

3. Next, embroider the leaves using four strands of DMC 3815 with satin stitch. To get the beautiful pointy shape, take a long center stitch and embroider two increasingly smaller stitches on each side, very close to each other. However, unlike the standard satin stitches that are parallel, these all will end in the same stitch hole near the stem.

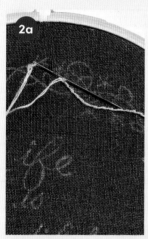

4. Embroider the berry stems with back stitch using four strands of DMC 833 and the berries themselves with French knots using six strands of DMC 3842 floss.

≈

5. To embroider the blue cornflowers, you need four strands of DMC 813. Take five small straight stitches in the shape of a star from a center point (much like you would make while embroidering the spoke for a woven wheel flower). Make another round of star-shaped stitches very close to the first stitches, but not quite on top of them. Finish with French knots in the center using four strands of DMC 833 floss.

≈

6. I always embroider the woven wheel close to the end of the project to reduce the risk of snagging your needle in the flowers! Embroider the flowers using four strands of DMC 3803 and DMC 3688, referring to the schematic.

7. Embroider the letters last; work small and neat back stitches using six strands of DMC 4150 along the shape of the letters, embroidering in a direction pretty much as you would if you were actually writing them. Keep the stitches around the curves very small so that you are able to capture the beautiful shapes of the letters.

8. When you've finished embroidering the pattern, remove any stabilizer or pen marks. If needed, wash, dry and refix the embroidery in your hoop and then close and back your hoop (see page 22 for instructions).

WELCOMING SPRING FLOWER BOUQUET

Difficulty Level: Easy

Stitches Used: Satin Stitch (page 29), French Knots (page 32), Back Stitch (page 27)

No embroidery experience is quite finished without a floral bouquet, is it? This is a beautiful pattern, simple but elegant, and uses the directionality of satin stitch (making different petals in different directions to give depth and perspective to a flower) wonderfully! I have used variegated (shaded) floss for one of the main elements, and it is such a wonderful way to show textures and depth of embroidery. We will also see what a huge difference filler flowers make! Those are the little flowers or French knots embroidered around a design to make it look "fuller."

This pattern would look wonderful on a little child's sweater or on the side of some table napkins with some extra filler flowers thrown in!

MATERIALS

- Lightboard, to transfer the pattern (optional)
- Transfer pen (white chalk pencil or white water-erasable pen)
- A minimum 7" (18-cm) square piece of light grey pure cotton or linen fabric
- 5" (13-cm) hoop with screws
- DMC 444 (Dark Lemon), 433 (Medium Brown), 915 (Dark Plum), 602 (Medium Cranberry), 731 (Dark Olive Green), 166 (Lime Green), 4120 (Tropical Sunset), 819 (Light Baby Pink), 3799 (Very Dark Pewter Grey)
- Size 3 and 5 embroidery needles (size 3 for French knots and size 5 for the rest of the stitches)
- Small embroidery scissors

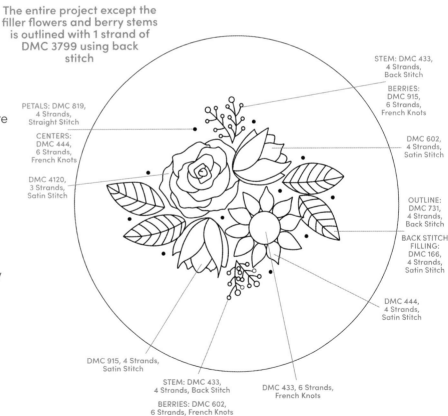

The entire project except the filler flowers and berry stems is outlined with 1 strand of DMC 3799 using back stitch

STEM: DMC 433, 4 Strands, Back Stitch

BERRIES: DMC 915, 6 Strands, French Knots

PETALS: DMC 819, 4 Strands, Straight Stitch

CENTERS: DMC 444, 6 Strands, French Knots

DMC 4120, 3 Strands, Satin Stitch

DMC 602, 4 Strands, Satin Stitch

OUTLINE: DMC 731, 4 Strands, Back Stitch

BACK STITCH FILLING: DMC 166, 4 Strands, Satin Stitch

DMC 444, 4 Strands, Satin Stitch

DMC 915, 4 Strands, Satin Stitch

STEM: DMC 433, 4 Strands, Back Stitch

DMC 433, 6 Strands, French Knots

BERRIES: DMC 602, 6 Strands, French Knots

1. Start by transferring the pattern and mounting the fabric on the hoop (refer to "Getting Started," [page 16]), making sure it's taut and the transferred pattern is centered.

❧

2. Begin by embroidering the petals of the sunflower with satin stitch using four strands of DMC 444. In a tear-shaped petal, always start the stitch from the center and work your way toward both ends. Embroider the center with French knots using six strands of DMC 433, outlining it first (with French knots).

❧

3. Embroider the tulip flowers next using four strands of DMC 915 and DMC 602 respectively, using the satin stitch and keeping the direction of the stitches true to the shape of the petals.

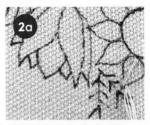

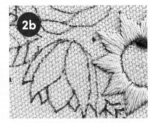

4. There are two ways to embroider the leaves. If you want the leaf accents to be highlighted, outline them first. However, if you want the body of the leaf to be the focus, embroider that first with satin stitch and fill in the accents later with back stitch. In this version, I have done the outlining first with back stitch using four strands of DMC 731. Next, fill in the leaf with satin stitch using four strands of DMC 166.

5. Next, embroider the rose with satin stitch using three strands of DMC 4120. I love embroidering roses with variegated floss because then all the variations of colors are achieved without any extra effort on my part! Embroider each adjacent pattern in a slightly different direction; this will give you that tightly wound effect of a real rose.

6. Embroider the stems next with back stitch using four strands of DMC 433 and the berries with six strands of DMC 602 and DMC 915 using French knots.

7.   Now that all the main elements are done, we come to the fun filler flowers! Embroider one round of the flower using four strands of DMC 819 in the shape of a star using straight stitch (variant of back stitch). Take five stitches in a different direction from the same center. Make another round of stitches overlapping the first five to give added depth to the flowers. Finish off the flowers with a French knot in the center using six strands of DMC 444.

8.   At this stage, your embroidery is technically complete and you are free to leave it as is. However, you can go one step further and outline the entire project with one strand of DMC 3799 floss.

9.   When you've finished embroidering the pattern, remove any stabilizer or pen marks. If needed, wash, dry and refix the embroidery in your hoop and then close and back your hoop (see page 22 for instructions).

SNOWY CHRISTMAS TREES

Difficulty Level: Intermediate

Stitches Used: Split Stitch (page 34), Running Stitch (page 26), Back Stitch (page 27), Herringbone Stitch (page 37), Satin Stitch (page 29), Fishbone Stitch (page 43), French Knots (page 32)

How fun is a winter landscape? In this project, you'll learn to embroider simple landscape shapes, especially trees. And because the trees are shaped as leaves—that's how you would see them from a distance, after all!—you can use any one of the same stitches when embroidering leaves in your future projects. I have kept the landscape shape very simple and accented it with a single line of running stitch. If you want it more detailed, feel free to use running stitch lines across the entire landscape (similar to the waves in Ocean Waves [page 53]). This is also the first project that uses metallic floss; it is fussier to use than cotton floss but has a wonderful visual effect. In the project steps, I have included tips and tricks that will help you embroider with it.

MATERIALS

- Lightboard, to transfer the pattern (optional)
- Transfer pen (white chalk pencil or white water-erasable pen)
- A minimum 7" (18-cm) square piece of light blue pure cotton or linen fabric
- 5" (13-cm) hoop with screws
- DMC 930 (Dark Antique Blue), 611 (Drab Brown), 700 (Bright Green), 522 (Fern Green), E703 (Light Emerald Green), 166 (Lime Green), 3346 (Hunter Green), 934 (Black Avocado Green), 17 (Light Yellow Plum), DMC 762 (Very Light Pearl Grey)
- Frixion Heat Erasable Pen or any water-erasable pen
- Size 3 and 5 embroidery needles (size 3 for metallic floss and French knots and size 5 for the rest of the floss/stitches)
- Small embroidery scissors

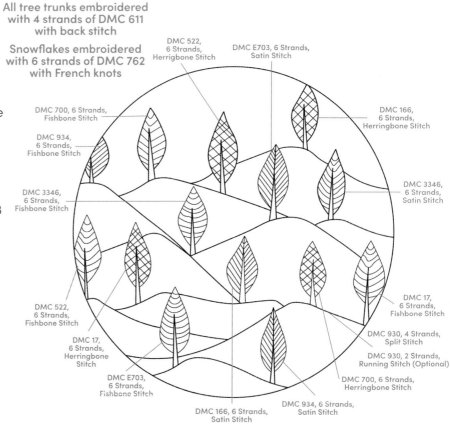

All tree trunks embroidered with 4 strands of DMC 611 with back stitch

Snowflakes embroidered with 6 strands of DMC 762 with French knots

DMC 522, 6 Strands, Herrigbone Stitch

DMC E703, 6 Strands, Satin Stitch

DMC 700, 6 Strands, Fishbone Stitch

DMC 166, 6 Strands, Herringbone Stitch

DMC 934, 6 Strands, Fishbone Stitch

DMC 3346, 6 Strands, Fishbone Stitch

DMC 3346, 6 Strands, Satin Stitch

DMC 17, 6 Strands, Fishbone Stitch

DMC 522, 6 Strands, Fishbone Stitch

DMC 930, 4 Strands, Split Stitch

DMC 17, 6 Strands, Herringbone Stitch

DMC 930, 2 Strands, Running Stitch (Optional)

DMC E703, 6 Strands, Fishbone Stitch

DMC 700, 6 Strands, Herringbone Stitch

DMC 166, 6 Strands, Satin Stitch

DMC 934, 6 Strands, Satin Stitch

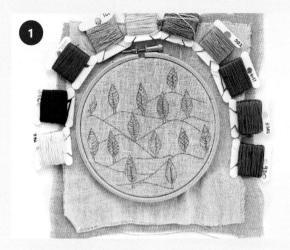

1. Start by transferring the pattern and mounting the fabric on the hoop (refer to "Getting Started" [page 16]), making sure it's taut and the transferred pattern is centered.

2. Begin embroidering the landscape mountains with split stitch using strands of DMC 930—add an accent with a single line of running stitch using two strands of the same floss. If you are not comfortable free-stitching the running stitch (simply keep the stitches parallel to the stitch line above), feel free to draw parallel lines with a Frixion pen underneath all the landscape mountains and then make running stitch on these.

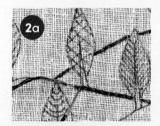
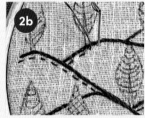

3. Next, proceed to embroider all the tree trunks with back stitch using four strands of DMC 611. Depending on which stitch we use to embroider the main body of the tree, some of the tree trunks will eventually be hidden, but you'll still be able to see them through the stitches, and that will add to the visual appeal.

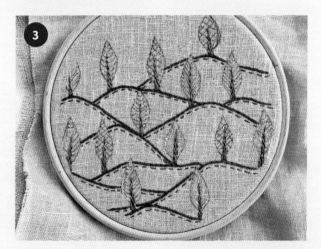

4. Referring to the schematic, begin embroidering the trees using six strands (except the metallic floss where I have used four strands) of different shades of green floss (DMC 700, DMC 522, DMC E703, DMC 166, DMC 3346, DMC 934 and DMC 17). I have used seven shades of greens to embroider fourteen trees, thus embroidering two trees with each of the floss numbers given above but using different stitches each time. This gives a beautiful effect because each stitch looks quite different with different colors. The only stitch with which you'll see the tree trunk fully is the satin stitch.

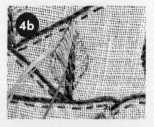

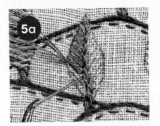

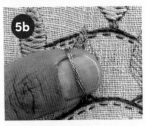

5. Although I have used six strands of cotton floss to embroider the trees, I have used only four strands of metallic floss (DMC E703), as it has greater volume than cotton floss. Always take two strands of the floss and double them over; this will give you greater control over the floss and help you flatten it as you stitch. One standard hurdle most stitchers face with metallic floss is that it tends to get knotted really easily while you're taking a stitch. What always helps me is to put your thumb between the floss and the fabric just before you end a stitch. Repeat the step when you are bringing the floss up after taking a stitch as well. This simple step will keep the floss flat against the fabric and you'll avoid all the knots!

6. Once you have stitched all the trees, your embroidery is already complete. However, you can add a snowy touch if you want to invoke the winter spirit! And it's easy to do this—simply take scattered French knots across the entire embroidery with six strands of DMC 762 floss (three strands of floss doubled over). Put them on the trees, in the air and on the ground. Bunch a few together. It's up to you how many or how few you embroider!

7. When you've finished embroidering the pattern, remove any stabilizer or pen marks. If needed, wash, dry and refix the embroidery in your hoop and then close and back your hoop (see page 22 for instructions).

PRETTY IN PASTEL RAINBOW

Difficulty Level: Intermediate

Stitches Used: Back Stitch (page 27), Bullion Knots (page 35)

No collection of embroidery patterns is complete without a rainbow-themed pattern. Rainbows are eternal favorites to embroider—and why not? They epitomize hope and cheer, and on top of it, they're incredibly easy to embroider! I have made this pattern deliberately neutral in its color theme—so it will be suitable for a person of any gender. Attached is also the entire alphabet in small and block letters so you can trace the name and/or age of the person to customize your design. This is a very simple pattern to execute; the only reason I have put the difficulty level as intermediate is because it is the first time you will be embroidering the bullion knot *and* the first time you will be tracing different letters onto your fabric to make a word. I hope you have lots of fun making this for a special loved one in your life—my daughter loves having her very own rainbow with her name up on her wall!

MATERIALS

- Lightboard, to transfer the pattern (optional)
- Transfer pen (white chalk pencil or white water-erasable pen)
- A minimum 7" (18-cm) square piece of white or light pastel pure cotton or linen fabric
- 4" (11-cm) hoop with screws
- DMC 834 (Very Light Golden Olive), 778 (Very Light Antique Mauve), 3782 (Light Mocha Brown), 452 (Medium Shell Grey), 524 (Very Light Fern Green), 29 (Eggplant), 169 (Pewter Grey), 3799 (Very Dark Pewter Grey)
- Size 5 embroidery needle
- Small embroidery scissors

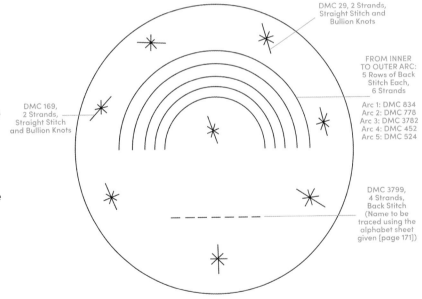

DMC 29, 2 Strands, Straight Stitch and Bullion Knots

FROM INNER TO OUTER ARC: 5 Rows of Back Stitch Each, 6 Strands

Arc 1: DMC 834
Arc 2: DMC 778
Arc 3: DMC 3782
Arc 4: DMC 452
Arc 5: DMC 524

DMC 169, 2 Strands, Straight Stitch and Bullion Knots

DMC 3799, 4 Strands, Back Stitch (Name to be traced using the alphabet sheet given [page 171])

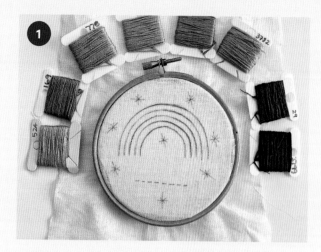

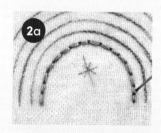
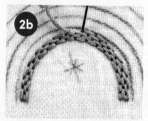
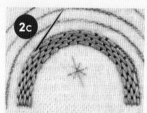
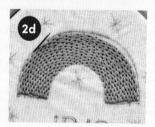

1.   Start by transferring the pattern and mounting the fabric on the hoop (refer to "Getting Started" [page 16]), making sure it's taut and the transferred pattern is centered.

2.   Embroider the rainbow following the schematic, starting at the innermost arc using six strands of DMC 834 using back stitch. When you begin to embroider the second line, start at a distance halfway along the second stitch of the first line. This will give a lovely brick effect in your back stitches. Continue making five rows of each color. Once you have embroidered with one color, move on to the next color in the schematic and following the same technique, embroider five more rows. Continue embroidering the entire rainbow in this manner using six strands of DMC 778, DMC 3782, DMC 452 and DMC 524.

3. Once the rainbow is embroidered, move on to the scattered stars, which we will embroider in two ways using two strands of DMC 29 and DMC 169. Some of the stars are embroidered with straight stitches (a simple variant of back stitch; see Fishy Playdate, page 56) along the pattern lines. For some stars, however, we will embroider two of the intersecting lines with bullion knots to give an additional textural effect. Because we want the knot to be a straight line, make sure to wrap the floss on the needle the same length as the length of the spoke of the star. The finished star will appear as a beautiful 3D shape.

4. Trace the name from the schematic given and embroider with two rows of back stitches along the pattern using four strands of DMC 3799 (you can use any other color of your choice here, too!). To give the brick-like effect, start the second line at 1½ stitches of the first line, the same as the rainbow.

5. When you've finished embroidering the pattern, remove any stabilizer or pen marks. If needed, wash, dry and refix the embroidery in your hoop and then close and back your hoop (see page 22 for instructions).

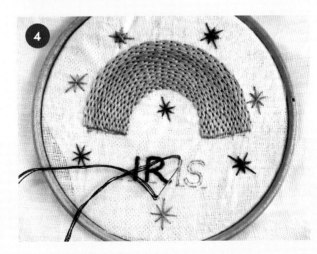

EMBROIDERED TWISTS FOR YOUR HOME AND APPAREL

FUNCTIONAL PATTERNS

How awesome is it to see something you have lovingly made become a functional item in your own home or gifted to a loved one? I firmly believe that embroidery is more than decorative art meant to be used as wall décor. For me, the best use of embroidery is to add beauty to items of daily use and uplift them! And don't worry, embroidery is not as fragile as it is reputed to be—with just a little care, you can use your embroidered homeware or apparel on a regular basis and still make them last years.

In this section, I take you through different projects embroidering homeware (like cushions, table runners and tote bags) and apparel (like jackets and baby clothes). My personal favorites are the tote bag and the little mushroom sweater! All these patterns can be interchanged or modified: use the Autumn Breath Tote Bag pattern (page 179) on a cushion and the Woodsy Toadstool Sweater pattern (page 185) on a tote. The transfer methods differ between a straightforward hoop and already-stitched homeware and apparel, so I will cover how to transfer patterns using wash-away stabilizers and tracing paper. I will also cover how to work with embroidery that is too big to fit all at once in your embroidery hoop. Finally, I will touch upon the best stitches to use and which to avoid when making a functional embroidered item.

Once you've completed your project, there are a few things to keep in mind to make your embroidered apparel and homeware last years! First of all, it is safe to wash your clothes in a gentle wash cycle (the one you use for your delicates and woolens). Always wash your clothes in a cloth bag; that way you protect them from zippers and hooks in other pieces of clothing. Avoid using the tumble dryer to dry your clothes—I always recommend air drying. Make sure you use good-quality, colorfast floss.

Although it is unlikely that the colors from the floss will run if you use good-quality branded floss, in case they do, I suggest using Dylon SOS Color Run (I have used this myself many times) or a similar color run fixer product. Dr. Beckmann, Carbona and Fabric Magic are a few other brands you could try.

I hope with the help of the patterns and guidance throughout this section, you will be able to fill your home and wardrobe with beautiful creations you have lovingly created with your own hands!

LOVIN' MY NEW DENIM JACKET

Difficulty Level: Intermediate

Stitches Used: Running Stitch (page 26), Chain Stitch (page 31), Stem Stitch (page 28), Split Stitch (page 34), Back Stitch (page 27), Satin Stitch (page 29), Stem Stitch Rose (page 40), Herringbone Stitch (page 37), French Knots (page 32), Woven Wheel Rose (page 38)

We now enter what I call the fun zone! Because from here on, and especially in this project, a lot of decisions about stitches and colors will be made by you. For this project, I have specially chosen a design that is very fluid; it's essentially just a bunch of different size circles. You may choose to fill up some of them with satin, chain or herringbone stitch. Give your jacket a textural spin using stem stitch roses or French knots! Make concentric circles using running stitch. Or simply outline them in chain stitch, back stitch or blanket stitch! Although I love using shades of blue on blue denim, feel free to use your own favorite palette and play around with different stitches. This is a safe design, and everything you make will look awesome! I have made the design so it can be fitted to an area of your choice—just add or reduce the circles you trace and you're good to go! I have used around sixteen shades of blue—you can get these exact shades, similar ones or a different palette altogether. Although there is a schematic attached, the intent is for you to play with different colors and stitches. However you go about this project, be assured you won't go wrong. Even if, at a halfway stage, you're not feeling too confident about how it is turning out, keep going and you'll be pleasantly surprised once finished!

MATERIALS

- Carbon paper, to transfer the pattern
- Transfer pen (White chalk pencil or white water-erasable pen for a dark-colored jacket; Frixion pen for a light-colored jacket)
- A denim jacket or shirt (You can also use a jacket or shirt of any other color/material)
- Embroidery hoop (6" or 7" [15 or 18 cm])
- DMC 4030 (Monet's Garden), 931 (Medium Antique Blue), 162 (Light Baby Blue), 4240 (Midsummer Night), 3846 (Light Bright Turquoise), White (Blanc), 3843 (Electric Blue), 4010 (Winter Sky), 820 (Very Dark Royal Blue), 311 (Medium Blue), 964 (Light Seagreen), 3761 (Light Sky Blue), 3807 (Cornflower Blue), 807 (Peacock Blue), 3842 (Dark Wedgewood), 4015 (Stormy Skies)
- Size 3 embroidery needle
- Small embroidery scissors

Fill the bigger circles entirely with running stitch.

Fill the smallest circles (unmarked) with either satin stitch, woven wheel rose or stem stitch rose. Use colors of your choice from the palette given.

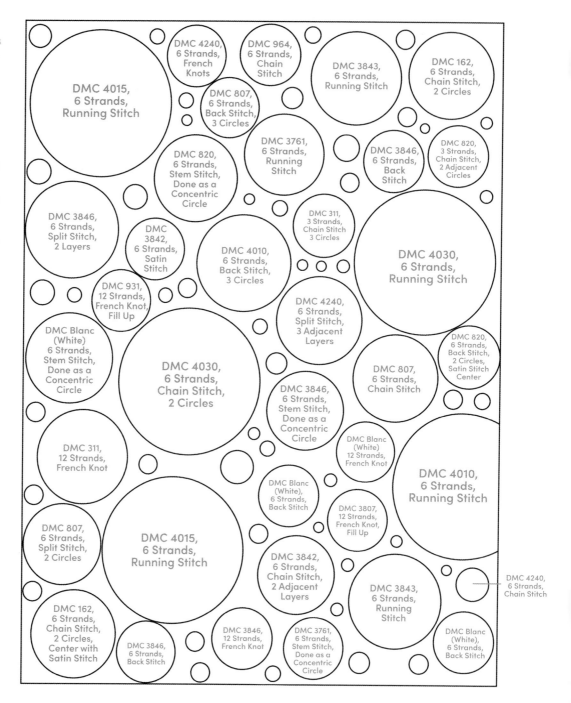

DMC 4240, 6 Strands, French Knots

DMC 964, 6 Strands, Chain Stitch

DMC 3843, 6 Strands, Running Stitch

DMC 162, 6 Strands, Chain Stitch, 2 Circles

DMC 4015, 6 Strands, Running Stitch

DMC 807, 6 Strands, Back Stitch, 3 Circles

DMC 3761, 6 Strands, Running Stitch

DMC 3846, 6 Strands, Back Stitch

DMC 820, 3 Strands, Chain Stitch, 2 Adjacent Circles

DMC 820, 6 Strands, Stem Stitch, Done as a Concentric Circle

DMC 3846, 6 Strands, Split Stitch, 2 Layers

DMC 3842, 6 Strands, Satin Stitch

DMC 4010, 6 Strands, Back Stitch, 3 Circles

DMC 311, 3 Strands, Chain Stitch 3 Circles

DMC 4030, 6 Strands, Running Stitch

DMC 931, 12 Strands, French Knot, Fill Up

DMC 4240, 6 Strands, Split Stitch, 3 Adjacent Layers

DMC 820, 6 Strands, Back Stitch, 2 Circles, Satin Stitch Center

DMC Blanc (White) 6 Strands, Stem Stitch, Done as a Concentric Circle

DMC 4030, 6 Strands, Chain Stitch, 2 Circles

DMC 3846, 6 Strands, Stem Stitch, Done as a Concentric Circle

DMC 807, 6 Strands, Chain Stitch

DMC 311, 12 Strands, French Knot

DMC Blanc (White) 12 Strands, French Knot

DMC 4010, 6 Strands, Running Stitch

DMC Blanc (White), 6 Strands, Back Stitch

DMC 3807, 12 Strands, French Knot, Fill Up

DMC 807, 6 Strands, Split Stitch, 2 Circles

DMC 4015, 6 Strands, Running Stitch

DMC 3842, 6 Strands, Chain Stitch, 2 Adjacent Layers

DMC 3843, 6 Strands, Running Stitch

DMC 4240, 6 Strands, Chain Stitch

DMC 162, 6 Strands, Chain Stitch, 2 Circles, Center with Satin Stitch

DMC 3846, 6 Strands, Back Stitch

DMC 3846, 12 Strands, French Knot

DMC 3761, 6 Strands, Stem Stitch, Done as a Concentric Circle

DMC Blanc (White), 6 Strands, Back Stitch

1. Start by transferring the pattern using carbon paper. If the schematic is smaller than the area of the jacket you want covered, you will have to add some extra circles all around to cover the area you need; embroider these using your instincts and the pointers I have shared in the following steps, if you're following the schematic for the rest. Mount the fabric on the hoop (refer to section "Getting Started" [page 16]), making sure it's taut. I also recommend redrawing the pattern with a white washable marker (if it's a dark color) or a Frixion pen (if it's a light color).

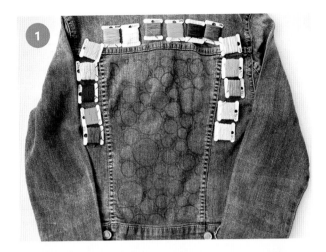

≫

2. There is no specific guideline on which order to follow while embroidering, but I recommend always embroidering your woven wheels and French knots last in any section of the fabric; because these are very textural 3D embroideries, they will interfere when you mount your fabric in a hoop or a frame. There is also the added risk of snagging or pulling the stitches in the process.

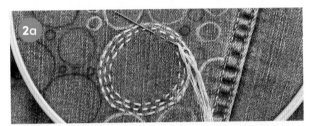

≫

3. Embroider the bigger circles with either running stitch or outline stitches, such as chain stitch, stem stitch, split stitch or back stitch. You can make a single outline border or even concentric circles or a whirlpool. Embroider the smallest circles with stitches you can fill in with; I have mainly used satin stitch, stem stitch rose and herringbone stitch.

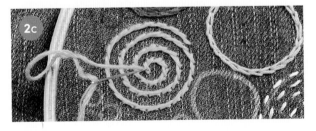

≫

4. While embroidering French knots, you can either do just one outline row along the perimeter or fill them in for a real pop.

5. Embroider the textural stitches (such as French knots, woven wheel rose and stem stitch rose) next to the circles where you have made outline stitches or filled with running stitch; this will give a contrast effect that will look beautiful from afar. Spread out your stitches—you have plenty to play around with—so even if you are filling your entire piece with only outline stitches, use different stitches in circles nearby. That will enhance the depth of your embroidery. Variegated floss can be used to amazing effect in embroideries such as these because they give an additional perspective.

6. I have also added a few scattered circles at the front—this is an optional step.

7. Once embroidered, remove the pen marks or stabilizer marks and, if needed, wash the garment in a gentle machine cycle. Leave it to air dry—iron on the back side to smooth the fabric.

BOHO BUDDIES CUSHION

Difficulty Level: *Easy*

Stitches Used: Chain Stitch (page 31), Back Stitch (page 27), Satin Stitch (page 29), Split Stitch (page 34), French Knots (page 32), Granitos Stitch (page 42)

I adore folksy patterns! First, because they are very cute. Second, because they're symbolic representations, you can really play around with the colors and embroideries without worrying about how "real" it will look. Third, they lend themselves to so many uses. For instance, this pattern would look equally cute mounted on a hoop or embroidered on a cushion. Feeling adventurous? Trace and embroider the individual flowers scattered across an apron or a dress! I promise you, they'll look gorgeous.

MATERIALS

- Any brand wash-away stabilizer, for transferring pattern
- Regular pencil or Frixion pen, to draw the pattern
- A cushion cover that's minimum 12" (30-cm) square or rectangle in a color of your choice (I have used a lime green 16" [40-cm] square linen cushion)
- 8" (20-cm) hoop with screws
- DMC 300 (Very Dark Mahogany), 4511 (Indian Summer), 166 (Lime Green), 730 (Very Dark Olive Green), 900 (Dark Burnt Orange), 902 (Very Dark Garnet), 742 (Light Tangerine), 956 (Geranium)
- Size 5 embroidery needle
- Small embroidery scissors

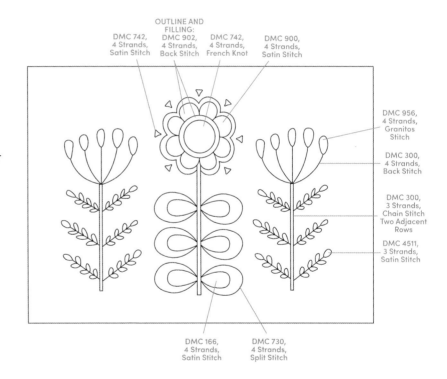

OUTLINE AND FILLING:
DMC 742, 4 Strands, Satin Stitch
DMC 902, 4 Strands, Back Stitch
DMC 742, 4 Strands, French Knot
DMC 900, 4 Strands, Satin Stitch

DMC 956, 4 Strands, Granitos Stitch

DMC 300, 4 Strands, Back Stitch

DMC 300, 3 Strands, Chain Stitch Two Adjacent Rows

DMC 4511, 3 Strands, Satin Stitch

DMC 166, 4 Strands, Satin Stitch

DMC 730, 4 Strands, Split Stitch

1. Start by transferring the pattern on the wash-away stabilizer, sticking the stabilizer on the right side of the fabric and then mounting the fabric on the frame (refer to "Getting Started" [page 16]), making sure it's taut and the transferred pattern is centered.

2. Embroider the three main stems using chain stitch in two rows using three strands of DMC 300. Make the stems for the buds using back stitch and four strands of DMC 300.

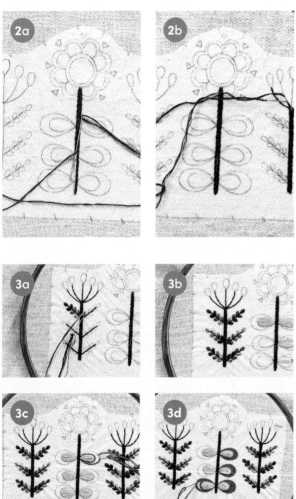

3. Make the leaves for both the stems on either side using satin stitch and three strands of DMC 4511; take a long stitch along the center of the leaf perpendicular to the shape. Take two or three stitches on each side, ending them close to where the leaf meets the stem. For the center stem, embroider the inside portion of the leaf using satin stitch and four strands of DMC 166. Because the leaf is a teardrop shape, you will need to taper some of the stitches on the narrower edge. Embroider the outer portion of the leaf with split stitch using four strands of DMC 730. Make both the outlines (inner and outer) first and then proceed to fill it up with the same stitch. When you fill up the inside of any element with satin stitch and then proceed to fill up the outer portion with a line stitch (chain, back or split stitch), it gives a beautiful "raised" effect to the overall embroidery.

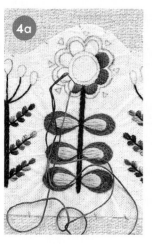

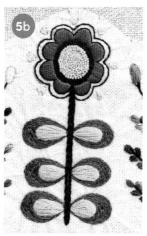

4. Make the petals of the flowers with satin stitch using four strands of DMC 900, beginning each petal from the center and proceeding to embroider each half of it. Embroider the outlines with back stitch using four strands of DMC 902, including the border around the center of the flower.

❧

5. Fill the center with French knots using four strands of DMC 742, first embroidering the outline and then proceeding to fill it up. Embroider the little triangles around the flower with satin stitch, again using four strands of DMC 742.

❧

6. Make the buds with granitos stitch using four strands of DMC 956, taking around eight to ten stitches for each bud. Once embroidered, remove the pen marks or stabilizer marks and, if needed, wash the garment in a gentle machine cycle. Leave it to air dry—iron on the back side to smooth the fabric.

❧

SPRINGING IT TABLE RUNNER

Difficulty Level: Easy

Stitches Used: Satin Stitch (page 29), Stem Stitch (page 28), French Knots (page 32), Chain Stitch (page 31), Split Stitch (page 34), Back Stitch (page 27)

For this adorable table runner, I have traced the pattern twice in succession to create a larger embroidery surface than what a single tracing would provide. You can, of course, do this for *any* pattern, especially those with scattered elements, as rearranging individual elements while tracing becomes easier. The best thing for me about this pattern? There are four distinct floral elements, and all these designs don't need an exact rendition, either of the tracing or the embroidery itself. After all, aren't sprigs of lavender in nature all different?

MATERIALS

- Lightboard, for transferring the pattern (optional)
- Transfer pen (white chalk pencil or white water-erasable pen)
- A pure cotton or linen table runner in a color of your choice (I have gone for a chocolate brown linen runner)
- 5" (13-cm) hoop with screws
- DMC White (Blanc), 444 (Dark Lemon), 780 (Ultra Very Dark Topaz), 29 (Eggplant), 3042 (Light Antique Violet), 734 (Light Olive Green), 3023 (Light Brown Grey), 3760 (Medium Wedgewood), 915 (Dark Plum), 3688 (Medium Mauve)
- Size 5 embroidery needle
- Small embroidery scissors

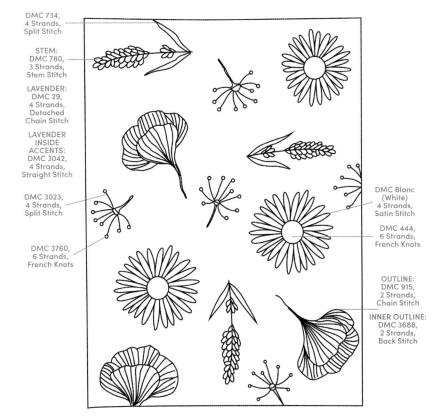

DMC 734, 4 Strands, Split Stitch

STEM: DMC 780, 3 Strands, Stem Stitch

LAVENDER: DMC 29, 4 Strands, Detached Chain Stitch

LAVENDER INSIDE ACCENTS: DMC 3042, 4 Strands, Straight Stitch

DMC 3023, 4 Strands, Split Stitch

DMC 3760, 6 Strands, French Knots

DMC Blanc (White), 4 Strands, Satin Stitch

DMC 444, 6 Strands, French Knots

OUTLINE: DMC 915, 2 Strands, Chain Stitch

INNER OUTLINE: DMC 3688, 2 Strands, Back Stitch

1. Start by transferring the pattern twice on the runner and mounting it on the hoop (refer to "Getting Started" [page 16]), making sure it's taut.

≫

2. Embroider the petals of the daisies with satin stitch using four strands of DMC White floss, beginning each petal from the center and working your way toward both ends. Once all the petals in a flower are embroidered, embroider the center using French knots and six strands of DMC 444, first outlining the center and then filling it in.

≫

3. Next, work on the lavender sprigs, first by embroidering the stems with stem stitch using three strands of DMC 780. Embroider the lavender buds using four strands of DMC 29 and making detached chain stitches along the shape—some of them will overlap, which will give a gorgeous 3D effect! Add the accents using four strands of a lighter shade of lavender (DMC 3042) using single straight stitches *inside* each of the detached chain stitches. Finish off with leaves embroidered with split stitch using four strands of DMC 734. Split stitch looks a lot like chain stitch, just a lot more slender.

≫

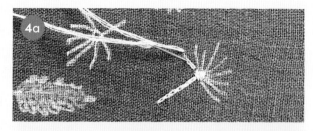

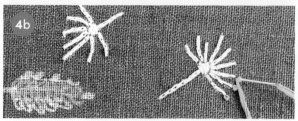

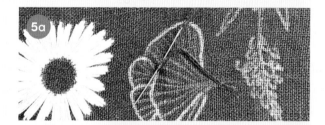

4. Embroider the dandelion stems next with split stitch using four strands of DMC 3023, and finish off with French knots using six strands of DMC 3760 at the tips.

≫

5. Finally, for the poppies, embroider the outlines with split stitch using two strands of DMC 915. Embroider the accents in the petals with back stitch using two strands of a lighter shade of pink (DMC 3688).

≫

6. Once embroidered, remove the pen marks or stabilizer marks and, if needed, wash the garment on a gentle machine cycle. Leave it to air dry—iron on the back side to smooth the fabric.

≫

AUTUMN BREATH TOTE BAG

Difficulty Level: Intermediate

Stitches Used: Back Stitch (page 27), Chain Stitch (page 31), Fishbone Stitch (page 43), Satin Stitch (page 29), French Knots (page 32), Soft Shading (page 46), Split Stitch (page 34), Granitos Stitch (page 42)

This is one of my favorite projects in this book, simply for all the textures it contains! Consider this your very own leaf sampler embroidery—and along with experimenting with leaves using different embroidery stitches, you get your very own leafy embroidered tote bag! I have included so many projects highlighting different floral elements, it just seemed right to have one where leaves are the *pièce de résistance*! In this pattern you will learn to embroider and fill leaves using a variety of stitches. Seeing them together is a good way to understand how textures and overall effects change with the stitches you use. You can easily use this design on a hoop, too; because they are individual elements, simply scatter a chosen number of them around in a hoop of your choice and add the filler berries and acorns in the extra space. In the steps below, I will cover the specific elements where you have to pay special attention while using certain stitches to get a great textural effect.

MATERIALS

- Lightboard or carbon paper, to transfer the pattern
- Transfer pen (Frixion pen or water-erasable pen in blue or black ink)
- A pure cotton or linen tote bag in a color of your choice
- A Q-snap frame or embroidery hoop with screws
- DMC 3031 (Very Dark Mocha Brown), 935 (Dark Avocado Green), 830 (Dark Golden Olive), 18 (Yellow Plum), 94 (Khaki Green), 3803 (Dark Mauve), 522 (Fern Green), 111 (Mustard), 368 (Light Pistachio Green), 4130 (Chilean Sunset), 3828 (Hazelnut Brown), 166 (Lime Green)
- Size 3 or 5 embroidery needle
- Small embroidery scissors

STEM: DMC 935, 4 Strands, Back Stitch

LEAVES: DMC 94, 3 Strands, Satin Stitch

BERRIES: DMC 3803, 4 Strands, French Knot

OUTLINE: DMC 935, 2 Strands, Back Stitch

FILLING: DMC 522, 2 Strands, Chain Stitch

LEAVES: DMC 18, 4 Strands, Fishbone Stitch

STEM: DMC 935, 4 Strands, Back Stitch

DMC 3031, DMC 3828, 4 Strands, Satin Stitch

STEM: DMC 3031, 4 Strands, Back Stitch

LEAVES: DMC 830, 4 Strands, Satin Stitch

STEM: DMC 3031, 4 Strands, Back Stitch

BERRIES: DMC 3803, 6 Strands, French Knots

STEM: DMC 830, 4 Strands, Back Stitch

OUTLINE: DMC 111, 3 Strands, Split Stitch

FILLING: DMC 368, 4 Strands, Satin Stitch

FILLING: DMC 111, 3 Strands, Long and Short Stitch

VEINS AND OUTLINE: DMC 935, 2 Strands, Back Stitch and Straight Stitch

OUTLINE: DMC 935, 4 Strands, Back Stitch

FILLING: DMC 3828, 4 Strands, Back Stitch

STEM: DMC 935, 4 Strands, Back Stitch

LEAVES: DMC 166, 4 Strands, Satin Stitch

VEINS: DMC 3031, 2 Strands, Chain Stitch

FILLING: DMC 4130, 3 Strands, Chain Stitch

STEM: DMC 3031, 4 Strands, Back Stitch

LEAVES: DMC 94, 3 Strands, Chain Stitch

STEM: DMC 3828, 4 Strands, Back Stitch

LEAVES: DMC 522, 4 Strands, Granitos Stitch

STEM: DMC 830, 4 Strands, Back Stitch

BERRIES: DMC 3803, 4 Strands, Satin Stitch

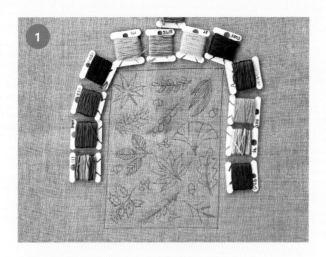

1. Start by transferring the pattern, making sure it's centered (refer to "Getting Started" [page 16]). For a stitched bag, flipping the pattern over is not an option. Hence you can directly trace the pattern without a hoop using a lightboard, or use a carbon transfer paper to trace the pattern with the fabric right side up. Mount the pattern on a hoop/frame (you don't need to cover the entire pattern in the hoop, just the portion you are embroidering).

2. When working on bigger projects, I prefer to embroider the stems all together because it helps give me an overall idea of how the colors will get placed. You may instead tackle individual elements if you like. In this project I have stitched the stems using back stitch and chain stitch using DMC 3031, DMC 935 and DMC 830 (refer to the Autumn Breath Tote Bag schematics, page 126).

3. **Element 1:** Embroider the stem using four strands of DMC 935 with back stitch. Consider this leaf as a bunch of seven leaves; stitch up each one using fishbone stitch with four strands of DMC 18, carefully ending each leaf at the center to get the wonderful textured veins. All fern-like leaves can be embroidered in this manner.

4. **Element 2:** Embroider the stem using four strands of DMC 935 with back stitch. This leafy branch is embroidered using satin stitch with three strands of DMC 94, except each of the leaves has a vein. So your stitch needs to start at the top of the leaf, and embroider using satin stitch on both ends. Make the berries with four strands of DMC 3803 using French knots.

∾

5. **Element 3:** For this cactus-like leaf, outline the entire leaf using back stitch with two strands of DMC 935, and then proceed to fill up the area inside using chain stitch with two strands of DMC 522. In some sections you may need two lines closely stitched together. If that makes the outlines blur out a little, don't worry! That will just add to the realistic look of the leaf.

∾

6. **Element 4:** Embroider the stem using back stitch with four strands of DMC 3031 and the berries using French knots with six strands of DMC 3803.

∾

7. **Element 5:** Embroider the stem with back stitch using four strands of DMC 3031 and stitch up the leaves using satin stitch with four strands of DMC 830.

∾

8. Element 6: For this fan-shaped leaf we will use soft shading with three strands of DMC 111, a variegated floss. The use of variegated floss is a smart move because it will give the natural color variations of a leaf without switching floss every little while. Begin by embroidering the outline using split stitch with three strands of DMC 111. Next, cover the sections of the leaf using soft shading stitches, taking long and short stitches in layers. The finished leaf shows the lovely shaded effect of a real autumn leaf.

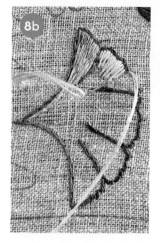

9. Element 7: Embroider the stem with four strands of DMC 830 using back stitch. Once the stem is done, unlike element 3, embroider the inner portion of the leaf first using satin stitch with four strands of DMC 368, keeping along the stitch lines. To finish the leaf, make the outline and inner leaf accents using back stitch with two strands of DMC 935. This is to make sure that the accents stand out clearly. If you want the accents to be muted, make the accents first using back stitch and then fill in the empty space using satin stitch.

10. Element 8: To embroider this gorgeous maple leaf, first embroider the veins with chain stitch using two strands of DMC 3031. Next, outline the entire leaf using chain stitch with three strands of DMC 4130, another variegated floss. Once the outline is done, proceed to fill in the inner area of the leaf with more chain-stitched lines taken close to the initial outline with the same floss.

11. Element 9: For this leaf, embroider the stem and veins with four strands of DMC 935 using back stitch. Outline the entire leaf, including the accents around the veins, with four strands of DMC 3828 using back stitch. Continue to fill in the shape of the leaf using more back stitch lines.

12. Element 10: Embroider the stem with back stitch using four strands of DMC 935. We are back to satin stitch for this leaf, which we will embroider with four strands of DMC 166. The only thing to keep in mind is that because the shape of the leaf is like a rose leaf (serrated on the edges), you need to alter the length of your stitches along the outer edge of the leaf.

13. **Element 11:** Embroider the stem with four strands of DMC 3828 using back stitch. This leaf stem is a fun one! Embroider it with the granitos stitch using four strands of DMC 522 to give it some lovely texture.

14. **Element 12:** The final leaf is the simplest of them all but packs a lovely effect. Embroider the stem with four strands of DMC 3031. Single chain stitches made with three strands of DMC 94 make up each leaf, and the use of shaded floss gives a lovely realistic effect to the whole branch.

15. **Filler Berries and Acorns:** The acorns are embroidered with satin stitches using four strands of DMC 3031 and DMC 3828. The berry stems are embroidered with back stitch using four strands of DMC 830, and the berries are embroidered with French knots using four strands of DMC 3803. You can add more of the fillers in your design if you wish to fill it up a little more.

16. Once embroidered, remove the pen marks or stabilizer marks and, if needed, wash the garment in a gentle machine cycle. Leave it to air dry—iron on the back side to smooth the fabric.

LOTUS OUTLINE PILLOWCASE

Difficulty Level: Easy

Stitches Used: Stem Stitch (page 28), Back Stitch (page 27)

This pattern is a classic example of how you can get a stunning result with just two stitches and three floss colors! This is such a simple design and yet you will get such a beautiful finish with this piece! What I love about this design is you can layer it like tiles to create a continuous big piece if you like. So feel free to trace and embroider an entire cushion with stem stitch outlines instead of just the center as I have done. Alternately, use only a portion to embroider in a hoop.

MATERIALS

- Wash-away stabilizer and lightboard, for transferring the pattern (optional)
- Transfer pen (Frixion Heat Erasable Pen or any water-erasable pen)
- A cushion in a color of your choice, preferably cotton or linen (I have used a cotton silk cushion in green)
- 5" (13-cm) hoop with screws
- DMC 4210 (Radiant Ruby), 3021 (Very Dark Brown Grey), 166 (Lime Green)
- Size 5 embroidery needle
- Small embroidery scissors

DMC 3021, 3 Strands, Stem Stitch

DMC 4210, 3 Strands, Stem Stitch

DMC 166, 3 Strands, Back Stitch

1. Start by transferring the pattern on the wash-away stabilizer, sticking the stabilizer on the right side of the fabric and then mounting the fabric on the frame (refer to "Getting Started" [page 16]), making sure it's taut. As an additional precaution to prevent the stabilizer from shifting, you can also take some outline running stitches along the edges.

⊱⊰

2. Begin embroidering the lotus flowers with three strands of DMC 4210 and using stem stitch; revisit the steps we covered in The Chakra Chronicles (page 61) to make sure you get the lotus petals sharp and well defined, all the while keeping the floss below the needle.

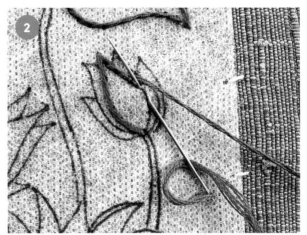

⊱⊰

3. Because the embroidery hoop will cover the entire project, you want to finish all the elements on one side before shifting the hoop to the other half of the pattern. Hence, embroider the stems using stem stitch with three strands of DMC 3021 alongside the flowers. Once one half is entirely embroidered, shift the hoop and embroider the other half.

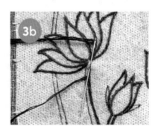

⊱⊰

4. Once all the outlines are done, fill in the stem accents with back stitch using three strands of DMC 166. If some portions of the stems are too thick to be filled with a single line of back stitch, embroider two parallel lines to fill it up.

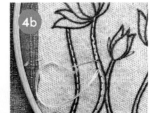

⊱⊰

5. Once embroidered, remove the pen marks or stabilizer marks and if needed, wash the garment in a gentle machine cycle. Leave it to air dry—iron on the back side to smooth the fabric.

FESTIVE FELT CHRISTMAS TREE ORNAMENT

Difficulty Level: Complex

Stitches Used: Split Stitch (page 34), Satin Stitch (page 29), Back Stitch (page 27), Chain Stitch (page 31)

This is a 2-in-1 project: You can make it as a Christmas hoop or turn it into an ornament for your tree! If you're embroidering on fabric, you won't need stabilizer to transfer the pattern—I use it for felt because it's difficult to trace fine details on felt directly. The pattern is quite easy to embroider, but the schematic is dense and detailed and there is the added step of finishing the raw edges, so I have marked it as complex.

MATERIALS

- Wash-away stabilizer and lightboard, for transferring the pattern (optional)
- Transfer pen (Frixion Heat Erasable Pen or any water-erasable pen)
- Two minimum 7" (18-cm) square pieces of light-colored felt, pure cotton or linen fabric (if you are not turning this into an ornament, one piece is enough)
- 5" (13-cm) hoop with screws
- DMC 3842 (Dark Wedgewood), 550 (Very Dark Violet), E815 (Dark Red Ruby), 700 (Bright Green), 166 (Lime Green), 915 (Dark Plum), E3821 (Light Gold), 973 (Bright Canary)
- Size 3 and 5 embroidery needles (size 3 for metallic floss and size 5 for other floss)
- Small embroidery scissors
- Pins (optional)
- Cotton stuffing or polyester fiberfill, to fill the ornament
- A small length of ribbon, to hang the ornament

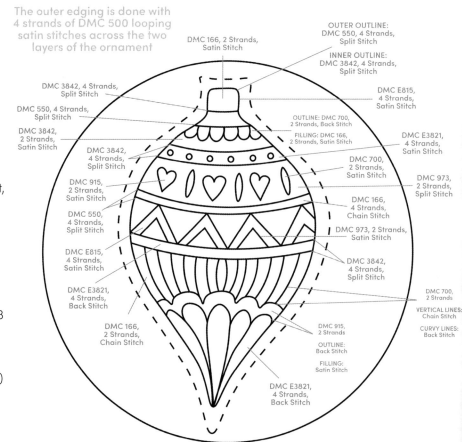

The outer edging is done with 4 strands of DMC 500 looping satin stitches across the two layers of the ornament

OUTER OUTLINE: DMC 550, 4 Strands, Split Stitch

INNER OUTLINE: DMC 3842, 4 Strands, Split Stitch

DMC 166, 2 Strands, Satin Stitch

DMC 3842, 4 Strands, Split Stitch

DMC 550, 4 Strands, Split Stitch

DMC 3842, 2 Strands, Satin Stitch

DMC 3842, 4 Strands, Split Stitch

DMC 915, 2 Strands, Satin Stitch

DMC 550, 4 Strands, Split Stitch

DMC E815, 4 Strands, Satin Stitch

DMC E3821, 4 Strands, Back Stitch

DMC 166, 2 Strands, Chain Stitch

DMC E815, 4 Strands, Satin Stitch

OUTLINE: DMC 700, 2 Strands, Back Stitch

FILLING: DMC 166, 2 Strands, Satin Stitch

DMC 700, 2 Strands, Satin Stitch

DMC E3821, 4 Strands, Satin Stitch

DMC 973, 2 Strands, Split Stitch

DMC 166, 4 Strands, Chain Stitch

DMC 973, 2 Strands, Satin Stitch

DMC 3842, 4 Strands, Split Stitch

DMC 700, 2 Strands

VERTICAL LINES: Chain Stitch

CURVY LINES: Back Stitch

DMC 915, 2 Strands

OUTLINE: Back Stitch

FILLING: Satin Stitch

DMC E3821, 4 Strands, Back Stitch

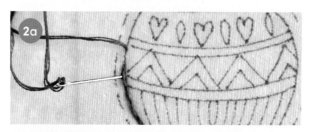

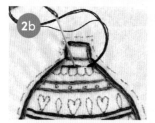

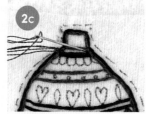

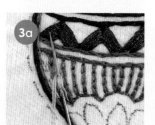

1. Start by transferring the pattern on the wash-away stabilizer, sticking the stabilizer on the right side of the fabric and then mounting the fabric on the frame (refer to "Getting Started" [page 16]), making sure it's taut and centered.

≈

2. In this project I have chosen to embroider different portions using the same color at the same time, as they occur across the design. Using split stitch, embroider the outlines (the inner outline with four strands of DMC 3842 and the outer outline with four strands of DMC 550). Alongside, also embroider the inner partition borders with the same floss numbers as per the schematic. Ignore the dotted outline drawing at this stage—that is simply a guideline to eventually cut your pattern when you make your ornament. Start by embroidering the portions with four strands of the red metallic floss (DMC E815) using satin stitch, as it is easier to fill in any gaps in the design with the nonmetallic floss.

≈

3. Embroider the portions with the greens (DMC 700 and DMC 166) next, using satin stitch, back stitch and chain stitch as per the schematic. Embroider the portions with plum (DMC 915) next, using back stitch and satin stitch with two strands of floss. Outline the little hearts first in back stitch and then fill them in with satin stitch. Doing that extra outline step with smaller shapes will ensure that the sharpness of the shape is captured.

≈

4. Fill in all the backgrounds with metallic gold (E3821, four strands), yellow (DMC 973, two strands), dark blue (DMC 3842, two strands) and plum (DMC 915, two strands) using split stitch and satin stitch, referring to the schematic. I chose to fill in the background of the hearts and petals with split stitch to navigate working around the odd shapes. Always fill in the background after embroidering the inner shapes, which will allow you to fill in any gaps left in the embroidery. If using the design as an embroidered hoop, you are done! The next steps are for turning it into an ornament.

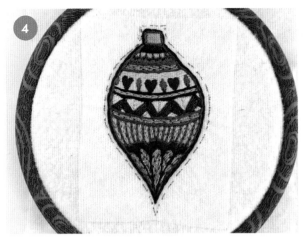

≫

5. Remove your embroidery from the hoop and cut along the outer border (that looks like a running stitch). Cut another felt piece in the same size and also get some filling material ready. You can hold both pieces of felt together with a pin or two. Start to fill in the raw edges with 4 strands of DMC 550 using satin stitch, but loop it across the two pieces of felt. Always use the same color as your outer border to help hide any stitches that are of an uneven length. Keep the stitches straight and very close to each other, making sure none of the felt shows through the stitches.

≫

6. When you are about to reach the top of the ornament, insert a loop of ribbon and take the next stitches through the ribbon to sew it into place. Continue filling in the raw edge in this fashion until you are about 1 inch (2.5 cm) from where you started off. Without snipping off the floss, add the filler material, filling as much as you can get in.

≫

7. Continue stitching until you have covered the entire ornament. Take a small knot and bring the floss out on the other side; pull it a little to give some tension and snip it off—the extra floss will hide inside the ornament and you won't see the jagged floss ends!

WOODSY TOADSTOOL SWEATER

Difficulty Level: Complex

Stitches Used: Soft Shading (page 46), Split Stitch (page 34), Back Stitch (page 27), French Knots (page 32), Chain Stitch (page 31), Satin Stitch (page 29)

This is the final project in the book, so it's just right we wrap it up with a bang! A lot of people think needle painting projects (realistic embroidery projects done usually with long and short stitch) are only for show on hoops. But I believe that they look just as beautiful on homeware and apparel, so I have made this cute mushroom project on a little girl's sweater! The process is the same should you want to make it on a hoop. This is the second project marked complex because it is done mostly with one or two strands of floss and thus is time consuming; however, give it a little patience and you will be amazed and proud of how far your embroidery skills have come!

MATERIALS

- Wash-away stabilizer and lightboard, for transferring the pattern (optional)
- Transfer pen (Frixion Heat Erasable Pen or any water-erasable pen)
- A minimum 7" (18-cm) square piece of light-colored pure cotton or linen fabric or a sweater for a little one
- 5" (13-cm) hoop with screws
- DMC 347 (Very Dark Salmon), 902 (Very Dark Garnet), 08 (Dark Driftwood), 07 (Driftwood), 730 (Very Dark Olive Green), 05 (Light Driftwood), 3864 (Light Mocha Beige), 436 (Tan), 310 (Black), 543 (Ultra Very Light Beige Brown), 166 (Lime Green), 600 (Very Dark Cranberry)
- Size 5 embroidery needle
- Small embroidery scissors

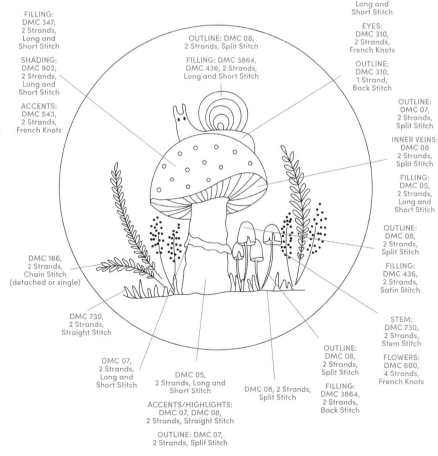

FILLING: DMC 347, 2 Strands, Long and Short Stitch

SHADING: DMC 902, 2 Strands, Long and Short Stitch

ACCENTS: DMC 543, 2 Strands, French Knots

OUTLINE: DMC 08, 2 Strands, Split Stitch

FILLING: DMC 3864, DMC 436, 2 Strands, Long and Short Stitch

DMC 08, 2 Strands, Long and Short Stitch

EYES: DMC 310, 2 Strands, French Knots

OUTLINE: DMC 310, 1 Strand, Back Stitch

OUTLINE: DMC 07, 2 Strands, Split Stitch

INNER VEINS: DMC 08 2 Strands, Split Stitch

FILLING: DMC 05, 2 Strands, Long and Short Stitch

OUTLINE: DMC 08, 2 Strands, Split Stitch

FILLING: DMC 436, 2 Strands, Satin Stitch

STEM: DMC 730, 2 Strands, Stem Stitch

FLOWERS: DMC 600, 4 Strands, French Knots

OUTLINE: DMC 08, 2 Strands, Split Stitch

FILLING: DMC 3864, 2 Strands, Back Stitch

DMC 08, 2 Strands, Split Stitch

DMC 166, 2 Strands, Chain Stitch (detached or single)

DMC 730, 2 Strands, Straight Stitch

DMC 07, 2 Strands, Long and Short Stitch

DMC 05, 2 Strands, Long and Short Stitch

ACCENTS/HIGHLIGHTS: DMC 07, DMC 08, 2 Strands, Straight Stitch

OUTLINE: DMC 07, 2 Strands, Split Stitch

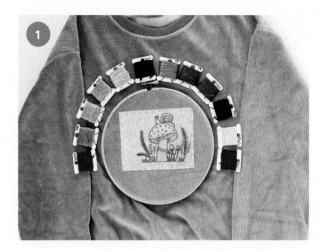

1. Start by transferring the pattern on the wash-away stabilizer, sticking the stabilizer on the right side of the fabric and then mounting the fabric on the frame (refer to "Getting Started" [page 16]), making sure it's taut and centered.

2. Needle painting takes time, but it is not as difficult as it looks in a finished embroidery. We will use two strands of DMC 347 and DMC 902 to embroider the mushroom cap with long and short stitches; start embroidering with layers of DMC 347. The stitches will fan out a little bit, and you shouldn't worry about a little distance between the stitches as that will get filled when you make the subsequent layers of stitches. Make a long stitch beneath each long stitch and a short stitch beneath each short one. Occasionally you may need to make extra adjacent stitches to help fan out the shape.

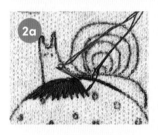

3. When you have filled up about 75 percent of the mushroom cap with DMC 347, embroider the bottom of the cap with the darker shade of red (DMC 902), again with long and short stitches. There should be space for one more layer of the lighter shade of red, so fill up the space again with long and short stitches with DMC 347.

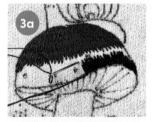
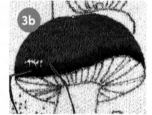

4. Now we move on to "blending"—while you can feel that the colors are merging, you want it to look even more natural—so take one strand of the darker red (DMC 902) and take long and short stitches where the layers merge.

5. Using split stitch and two strands of floss, embroider the underside veins with DMC 08 and outline the stem of the mushroom with DMC 07. Make the stems of the foliage and grass with stem stitch and back stitch respectively, using two strands of DMC 730 while referring to the schematic. Embroider the ground line with split stitch using two strands of DMC 08.

6. Fill the underside of the mushroom with split stitch using two strands of DMC 05. Fill in the stalk using long and short stitches, again with two strands of DMC 05. Leave the central knobby part of the mushroom stalk for last, and embroider that using long and short stitches in two layers with two strands of DMC 07. Add accents with two strands of DMC 07 and DMC 08 using straight, scattered stitches.

7. Embroider the body of the snail and the outline of its shell with two strands of DMC 08 using split stitch. Fill in the shell layers alternately with two strands of DMC 3864 and DMC 436 using split stitch.

8. Outline the smaller mushrooms (including stem) with DMC 08 using back stitch. Fill them in with satin stitch using two strands of DMC 3864 and DMC 436.

9. Outline the body of the snail with back stitch and make its eyes using French knots using two strands of DMC 310. Add the accent dots on the mushroom cap using French knots with two strands of DMC 543. That concludes the main elements of our needle painting: the mushrooms and the snail.

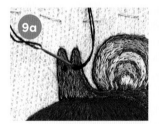

10. Next, embroider the leaves of the fern using chain stitch and two strands of DMC 166. To finish off the piece, embroider the floral elements using French knots and four strands of DMC 600. Once embroidered, remove the pen marks or stabilizer marks and, if needed, wash the garment on a gentle machine cycle. Leave it to air dry—iron on the back side to smooth the fabric.

PATTERNS

Patterns—along with schematics—are not the most interesting aspects of embroidery to look at, but they are really your best friends in disguise. Like I have mentioned before, use patterns as guidelines on how you want your design to be. So for the Autumn Breath Tote Bag project (page 125), you can choose to trace your leaves far apart and give them a more scattered look. Or just embroider individual elements (as in Fishy Playdate [page 56]) as patches.

The schematics, meanwhile, are what you will constantly refer to for guidance on stitches, floss colors and number of strands, especially in the more complex projects. In this book, they can be found alongside their respective projects.

While I have done all the embroideries in this book with six-stranded floss, you can easily substitute with Pearl Cotton No. 8 of the same shade numbers. The textures would be slightly different with Pearl cotton floss. Single-strand Pearl cotton floss consists of two strands of stranded floss. Two-strand Pearl cotton floss consists of four strands of stranded floss.

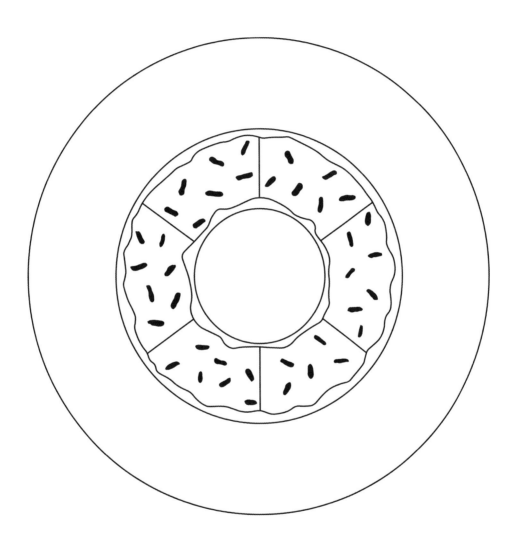

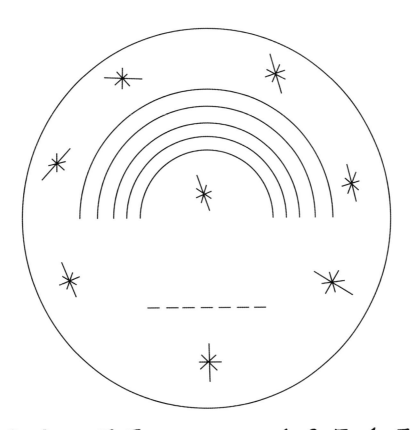

A B C D E F
G H I J K L
M N O P Q R
S T U V W X
Y Z

1 2 3 4 5 6
7 8 9 0
a b c d e f g
h i j k l m n
o p q r s t u
v w x y z

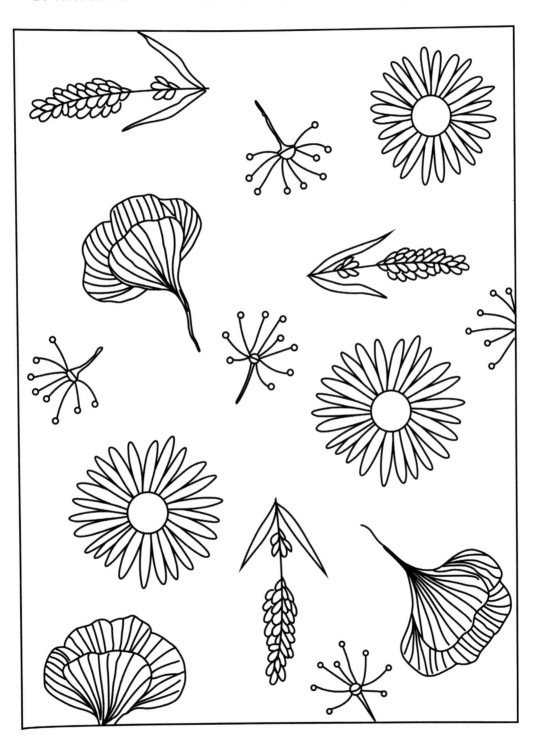

ACKNOWLEDGMENTS

I would like to thank Page Street Publishing, with a special mention of my wonderful editors Caitlin Dow and Sarah Monroe and their entire team, for giving me the opportunity to create this book. It was such a roller coaster navigating the various stages of book writing while coordinating different aspects of the process from across the ocean! I will always have wonderful memories of my association with the wonderfully talented and ever-supportive team at Page Street!

I would also like to give a high five to my three pillars of support—my husband, Himanshu, who believed I could do this more than I did myself, and my two darlings, Keshav and Kaveri. They found the work that goes into writing just one book mind-boggling! To be honest, so did I! This entire journey would not have been half as fun and fulfilling without their constant cheerleading.

To my dad, who didn't have a "crafty" eye, but who used to purchase my embroidery supplies and get patterns printed for me from my hometown. He would get them to wherever I was living in India at the time!

Thank you, Meghan and Chris, for the wonderful photography on the final projects and to Jessica Porter from DMC for kindly supplying me with the bulk of the material I have used to create the projects.

I would also like to mention my dear friend Sherry, who was my forever-present creative sounding board, both while developing and executing the various projects! Our detailed discussions made all the projects come alive in my mind.

Finally, I would like to thank my family and friends for their ever-present well wishes.

ABOUT THE AUTHOR

Dhara Shah has entered into the creative world of embroidery from a very different background. She has a bachelor's degree in engineering and a master's degree in business administration and has put ten years as an HR partner with IBM Global Services behind her. It was the premature birth of her second child, a daughter, that prompted her to take a break from the corporate world. Along the way, the child was diagnosed with mild autism, which further cemented Dhara's resolve to stay in close proximity to her. Somewhere along the way, Dhara rekindled her old love for embroidery and it turned into a full-fledged flame. Having ventured into the dizzying world of Instagram, Dhara found a wonderful community of like-minded artists and crafters and found her escape as well as a platform to showcase what she was creating. Like life, Dhara's embroidery journey has also developed and received support from the most unlikely sources, the most recent adventure being this wonderful opportunity to share her experience and knowledge with others who want to embark on a new hobby. She hopes to be able to keep creating and helping others along their creative journey!

You can find her designs in her Etsy shop: www.etsy.com/uk/shop/ChainStitchStore.

Dhara loves working with bright colors and draws inspiration from her surroundings as well as her roots back in India. If you would like to find out more, check out her Instagram where she regularly posts about her current projects and updates: http://www.instagram.com/chain_stitch.

INDEX